Onlin

Access landmark case law~ ~~ ~
case studies will give you an in-depth understa.....
The case studies included are:

1. Marbury vs Madison

2. Gibbons vs Ogden

3. Corwin v. KKR Fin. Holdings LLC

4. Boilermakers Local 154 Ret. Fund v. Chevron Corp.

5. Lieberman v. Wyo..com Ltd. Liab. Co.

6. GreenHunter Energy, Inc. v. W. Ecosystems Tech., Inc.

7. Boechler, P.C. v. Comm'r,

8. Liebeck v. McDonald's Restaurants 1995

9. United States v. Carroll Towing Co.

10. Encino Motorcars, LLC v. Navarro

11. Genesis Healthcare v. Symczyk

12. TransUnion LLC v. Ramirez

13. Salzberg v. Sciabacucchi

14. Walters v Morgan (1861) 3 De Gex, Fisher & Jones 718; 45 ER 1056.

15. Bartenwerfer v. Buckley

16. Marrama v. Citizens Bank

17. State St. Bank & Tr. Co. v. Signature Fin. Grp.

18. Quanta Comput., Inc. v. LG Elecs., Inc.

To access the case studies, follow the steps below:

1. Go to **www.vibrantpublishers.com**

2. Click on the **'Online Resources'** option on the Home Page

3. Login by entering your account details (or create an account if you don't have one)

4. Go to the Self-Learning Management series section and click on the **'Business Law Essentials You Always Wanted To Know'** link and access the templates.

Happy self-learning!

SELF-LEARNING MANAGEMENT SERIES

BUSINESS LAW ESSENTIALS

YOU ALWAYS WANTED TO KNOW

A simple, comprehensive, and useful guide about the laws that impact businesses in the US

KOMAL SHAH

Business Law Essentials
You Always Wanted To Know

First Edition

Paperback ISBN 10: 1-63651-170-8
Paperback ISBN 13: 978-1-63651-170-2

Ebook ISBN 10: 1-63651-171-6
Ebook ISBN 13: 978-1-63651-171-9

Hardback ISBN 10: 1-63651-172-4
Hardback ISBN 13: 978-1-63651-172-6

Library of Congress Control Number: 2023935585

This publication is designed to provide accurate and authoritative information in regard to the subject matter covered. The Author has made every effort in the preparation of this book to ensure the accuracy of the information. However, information in this book is sold without warranty either expressed or implied. The Author or the Publisher will not be liable for any damages caused or alleged to be caused either directly or indirectly by this book.

Vibrant Publishers books are available at special quantity discount for sales promotions, or for use in corporate training programs. For more information please write to bulkorders@vibrantpublishers.com

Please email feedback / corrections (technical, grammatical or spelling) to spellerrors@vibrantpublishers.com

To access the complete catalogue of Vibrant Publishers, visit www.vibrantpublishers.com

SELF-LEARNING MANAGEMENT SERIES

TITLE	PAPERBACK* ISBN
ACCOUNTING, FINANCE & ECONOMICS	
COST ACCOUNTING AND MANAGEMENT ESSENTIALS	9781636511030
FINANCIAL ACCOUNTING ESSENTIALS	9781636510972
FINANCIAL MANAGEMENT ESSENTIALS	9781636511009
MACROECONOMICS ESSENTIALS	9781636511818
MICROECONOMICS ESSENTIALS	9781636511153
PERSONAL FINANCE ESSENTIALS	9781636511849

ENTREPRENEURSHIP & STRATEGY	
BUSINESS PLAN ESSENTIALS	9781636511214
BUSINESS STRATEGY ESSENTIALS	9781949395778
ENTREPRENEURSHIP ESSENTIALS	9781636511603

GENERAL MANAGEMENT	
BUSINESS LAW ESSENTIALS	9781636511702
DECISION MAKING ESSENTIALS	9781636510026
LEADERSHIP ESSENTIALS	9781636510316
PRINCIPLES OF MANAGEMENT ESSENTIALS	9781636511542
TIME MANAGEMENT ESSENTIALS	9781636511665

*Also available in Hardback & Ebook formats

SELF-LEARNING MANAGEMENT SERIES

TITLE	PAPERBACK* ISBN
HUMAN RESOURCE MANAGEMENT	
DIVERSITY IN THE WORKPLACE ESSENTIALS	9781636511122
HR ANALYTICS ESSENTIALS	9781636510347
HUMAN RESOURCE MANAGEMENT ESSENTIALS	9781949395839
ORGANIZATIONAL BEHAVIOR ESSENTIALS	9781636510378
ORGANIZATIONAL DEVELOPMENT ESSENTIALS	9781636511481

MARKETING & SALES MANAGEMENT	
DIGITAL MARKETING ESSENTIALS	9781949395747
MARKETING MANAGEMENT ESSENTIALS	9781636511788
SALES MANAGEMENT ESSENTIALS	9781636510743
SERVICES MARKETING ESSENTIALS	9781636511733

OPERATIONS & PROJECT MANAGEMENT	
AGILE ESSENTIALS	9781636510057
OPERATIONS & SUPPLY CHAIN MANAGEMENT ESSENTIALS	9781949395242
PROJECT MANAGEMENT ESSENTIALS	9781636510712
STAKEHOLDER ENGAGEMENT ESSENTIALS	9781636511511

*Also available in Hardback & Ebook formats

About the Author

Komal Shah has worked for over 20 years in the domains of corporate law and corporate governance in various in-house roles. After qualifying her law and company secretaryship in India, Komal led the initial public offering of India Infoline Limited as its company secretary and compliance officer. Later, she moved to Dublin, Ireland, where she worked in various roles in the corporate governance function with a carbon credits trader called EcoSecurities (where she was managing the compliance for subsidiary entities located in 19 countries of the globe, including the United States) and BFSI entities such as DEPFA Bank, Citibank, and Northern Trust. After moving back to India, she headed and scaled the content function at LawSikho, a legal ed-tech company providing high-quality legal learning courses. She curated and created courses in international law and particularly US law based courses in this function. She was elevated to the position of a Co-founder for her contribution. Currently, she leads the business legal clinic for LawSikho where she helps early-stage startups with their contracts and compliance, while at the same time enabling students of LawSikho to work and develop hands-on expertise in international contract drafting and compliance-related work. She has helped numerous startups located in India, US, UAE, Singapore, Australia and other countries with respect to their contracts, entity formation in the US, flipping, acquisitions, corporate structuring and investment transactions.

This page is intentionally left blank

Table of Contents

7   Intellectual Property Law and Intellectual Property Registrations   121

8   Data Protection and Privacy Laws   143

12 Bankruptcy Laws   227

This page is intentionally left blank

Preface

Often founders wonder why they should know about the laws impacting their business. Wouldn't it be better to simply hire a lawyer to take care of the legal requirements? But here's the thing: availing specialized legal services is expensive and finding reliable legal services is difficult. Even when you hire a lawyer, you need to be aware of what it is that you need them to do for you. If you don't even know that, then you may be billed significantly high since you are expecting the lawyer to think and strategize for you.

This is why, it is essential to gain at least an overview of the laws that impact your business, and the laws that you may need to resort to while dealing with other persons or companies. It is not necessary that you become a lawyer or a legal expert, but it is necessary to gain a basic understanding of the laws you need to comply with, which actions you can become liable for, and what rights you have against a counterparty as a business owner.

Business Law Essentials You Always Wanted To Know (Business Law Essentials) gives you a comprehensive overview of all laws that you may become subject to, in the course of carrying on and running a business. It starts by explaining what a legal system is and the type of legal system that is followed in the US, the different forms of business organizations available as well as laws that would be applicable to an ongoing business, even in very early stages such as taxation, employment laws, intellectual property laws and so on. It even includes a basic understanding of bankruptcy laws, just in case a founder discovers down the road that a business is not viable.

The language used in the book has intentionally been kept free from legalese and at times, conversational, to ensure a simple explanation of the purpose behind a specific law and how it impacts day-to-day transactions. It does not get into complicated details and interpretations like a legal book but explains the impact of laws like a business book. I hope that it will be an effortless read.

Introduction to the book

The gamut of laws that can become applicable to a business can overwhelm a business owner. A prime principle of compliance with the law is that ignorance of the law is not an excuse and therefore, non-compliance can land a business heavy penalties.

Business Law Essentials moves along the stages which a business may pass through and deals with different laws which are relevant at different stages. It provides a basic idea about how businesses can be formed, and laws surrounding essential ingredients for the operation of businesses such as taxation, intellectual property, employment law, contracts, etc. As most businesses in today's world are either technology-based or have a tech front, an introduction to data protection and privacy laws has also been included. As businesses grow, factors such as the purchase of real estate, the possibility of actions by customers, and issues of securities to investors become relevant and therefore, this book covers those factors as well. Last, but not least, it also covers bankruptcy laws which can help determine what needs to be done in the event a business does not succeed.

After reading this book, you should be able to answer the below questions for yourself:

- What are the available forms of business in the US and what is the form your business should take?

- Which taxes are applicable to your business and which tax registrations do you require?

- How can you protect your brand - how can it be registered as intellectual property?

- What makes a contract valid and which laws are applicable to different types of contracts?

- What types of employment laws are you required to comply with?

- What kind of laws are you required to comply with when you want to issue securities?

How to use this book?

This book can be used to gain an initial understanding of the laws applicable to a business. The chapters in this book are deep enough to merit an independent book in itself. However, this book attempts to introduce you to the laws that affect businesses in the US.

1. Use this book to gain a general idea about business laws in the US. At times in the book, you will also discover the logic behind why a specific law was enacted and the purpose it serves.

2. Use this book as an applicability guide - it can help you know which laws apply to you and when.

3. Use this book not as a "be all and end all" for laws in a specific area, but as an introduction and a mechanism to know where to find more information, in case you need to go deeper within a specific area of law or if you need to find the laws applicable to multiple states.

4. Lastly, you can also use this book to correlate and gain an idea of the areas in which your business can be regulated, in case you wish to search for applicable laws in different countries.

This page is intentionally left blank

Who can benefit from this book?

1. Existing or potential founders can benefit from this book by knowing the legal environment surrounding their business. They can determine certain things in advance such as a possible form or applicable taxation and determine accordingly when and how they should proceed with the business.

2. Employees working with business organizations can be aware of the laws impacting the business and help in complying with such laws or at the very least, informing the management of the applicability.

3. Lawyers in other countries can be aware of the basics of US law and be able to guide businesses in those countries which are looking to expand to the US.

4. This book can also help to be a good book for law students and legal enthusiasts in different countries to read and understand the laws of the US.

This page is intentionally left blank

Chapter **1**

Legal System in the United States

You must have come across the names of different laws in the US at some point in time somewhere, maybe in some blogs or tweets or news. For example, the Jumpstart Our Business Startups (JOBS) Act or the Sarbanes - Oxley (SOX) Act. Did you know that all these laws work under a legal system? Or that there is a hierarchy of courts that you need to approach, in that order, if you need to file a suit? This chapter will introduce you to the basics of the legal system prevalent in the US, inform you about the role of the Constitution in the US legal system, as well as introduce you to the hierarchy of courts. The purpose of this chapter is to familiarize you with how any law in the US is interpreted and enforced. Read on!

Key learning objectives of this chapter include the reader's understanding of the following:

- What are the different types of legal systems and which legal system does the US follow?

- What role does the US Constitution play in the legal system?

- What is the difference between federal and state laws?

- Where can you find the business laws of a state?

- What are the different types of courts which you can find in the US and when to approach which court?

- Are there any laws in the US governing ethics and social responsibility?

1.1 Different Types of Legal Systems and the Legal System Prevalent in the United States

Let's first examine what a legal system is. *A legal system is a set of basic principles that are used in order to interpret the written laws.* Laws may be written in a specific language, but when it comes to applying the written laws to an actual situation, a nation's courts will consider the legal system being followed in that country.

The two main legal systems prevalent in the world are civil law and common law. To put it simply, a legal system based on civil law follows the letter of the written law. Therefore, the interpretation by the courts is more static and is not evolving. On the other hand, common law jurisdictions give significant consideration to judicial precedents i.e. how a previous case was decided while interpreting a particular law. Common law interpretations can therefore evolve because each subsequent decision becomes a reference point for future cases.

There can be legal systems based on religious law and customary practices also. However, these are not as prevalent as the above two systems.

Common law has its origins in England, and since historically, America was comprised of British colonies,[1] the US largely follows a common law legal system. The only exception is the state of Louisiana,[2] which was historically a French colony and thus, has a civil-law-based legal system.

1.2 The US Constitution and How It Impacts the Legal System

The US Constitution is the world's longest-surviving written charter of government.[3] It is divided into seven articles, which are further divided into different sections. It sets out which parts of the government exercise the legislative, the executive, and the judiciary functions in the US, what constitutes treason in the

1. Country Summary, United States, *The World Factbook*, CIA, https://www.cia.gov/the-world-factbook/countries/united-states/summaries/

2. John C. Henegan, Brian C. Kimball and Caroline Smith, Butler Snow LLP, *Legal Systems in the United States: Overview*, Thomson Reuters Practical Law https://uk.practicallaw.thomsonreuters.com/w-019-5918?transitionType=Default&con textData=(sc.Default)&firstPage=true, http://www.legis.la.gov/legis/Laws_Toc.aspx?folder=67&level=Parent

3. *Constitution of the United States*, United States Senate https://www.senate.gov/civics/constitution_item/constitution.htm

US, how can the Constitution be amended, how a new state can be added, and other powers and limitations on the US federal government.

 Did you know?

Before 2022, the last amendment to the US Constitution was the twenty-seventh amendment, made in 1992. It prohibited the implementation of laws varying the compensation for the services of Senators and Representatives until an election of Representatives intervened.

Some interesting sections of the US Constitution can be noted as under:

- The Congress, consisting of the Senate and the House of Representatives has all the legislative powers in the US. In the Senate, every state gets two Senators, regardless of population. No state gets a fixed number of representatives in the House of Representatives, because these are recalculated every ten years, based on the population of the state.

- Legislation, or "Bills", are passed through the Senate and the House of Representatives and thereafter signed by the President, in order to have the effect of law in the US.

- Though the executive power is vested in the President, the Congress has a lot of powers. These powers include levying and collecting taxes, borrowing money, regulating commerce with foreign nations, coining money, declaring war, etc.

- While the Constitution provides for the establishment of one Supreme Court, the Congress also has the power to establish inferior courts.

- The US follows the jury system for criminal trials, as against a trial by a judge. A trial by a judge is generally prevalent in countries that follow the civil law system.

- The fact that the legal system in the US is based on common law can be known from Article IV, Section 1 of the Constitution of the US, which states that "Full Faith and Credit shall be given in each state to the public Acts, Records and **judicial proceedings** of every other state."

1.3 Federal and State Laws

Federal laws apply to the whole of the US and are enacted, as stated above, when a bill is passed by both houses of the Congress and signed by the President.

Since the US follows a federal system, each of the states has its own constitution, governor, and bicameral legislatures (except Nebraska, which has a single house or unicameral legislature). State laws have the force of law only within the relevant state, and are enacted when a legislative bill is passed by the State Senate and State Legislative Assembly and signed into law by the governor of that state.

 For example, you can read about the constitution, legislature, executive, and judicial functions of the state of California here: www.loc.gov.

Did you know?

After the original nine states signed to give effect to the US Constitution, Delaware was the first state to ratify the US Constitution on December 7, 1787.

1.4 The Hierarchy of Courts in the United States

Let's assume that you own a business in California and you entered into a contract with someone to provide certain services. You completed the work for them and now, you are not getting paid for the work despite having tried everything to arrive at a resolution for a long time. Can you sue them? In which court will you file a suit? A breach of contract (someone not doing what they promised to do in a contract) can be one of the most common reasons why a small business owner would need to approach the judicial system. It is important to have an idea of the court system in the US for this purpose.

Figure 1.1

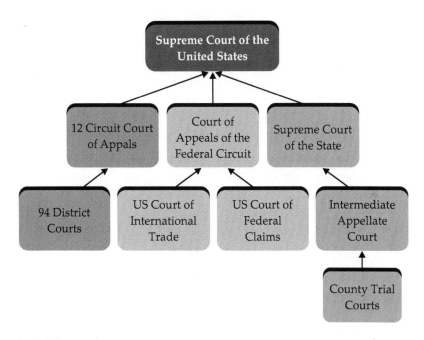

1.4.1 State Courts

In most cases, the first level of courts that you would approach is the State Courts.[4] If you are suing someone from a different state or suing over a federal law, you would start in Federal Court. The types of Courts found in different states are not the same and you can find different types of courts in each state. However, the system is substantially similar and the two main types of courts that you would find are Trial Courts and Appellate Courts. Each state also has its own Supreme Court.

---

4. State Court Websites, National Center for State Courts https://www.ncsc.org/information-and-resources/state-court-websites

1.4.2 Trial Courts

As the name suggests, these are the courts where a suit is originally filed and the trial is conducted. These can be further categorized as District Courts or Superior Courts and courts created for dealing with specific matters such as Small Claims, Probates, Bankruptcy, Juvenile matters, Family, Water, etc. Further, in some states such as California, there are County, Town, and Village Courts as well, which are trial courts.

In our above example of non-payment on a contract, you could file an action in a Small Claims court in California,[5] where you can sue and represent yourself for a contract value of up to $10,000.

1.4.3 Intermediate Appellate Courts

Where there are trial courts smaller than the District Court or Superior Court, such as a County Court, some states also have intermediate appellate courts. Appeals from the decisions of the smaller trial courts can be instituted in the intermediate appellate courts and appeals from the decisions of the intermediate appellate courts can be instituted in the Supreme Court for the state.

In other words, the District or Superior Courts are the highest trial courts and the Supreme Court is the highest appellate court in a state.

---

5. *Small Claims in California,* California Courts Self-help Guide, Judicial Branch of California, https://www.courts.ca.gov/1256.htm

1.4.4 Federal Courts

The US judicial districts are divided into 12 circuits and each of these circuits has a Court of Appeals. These Courts of Appeals hear appeals from the decisions of the District Courts or the Superior Courts i.e. the highest trial courts in the state falling within the realm of the specific circuit.

In addition, the United States Court of Appeals for the Federal Circuit has the jurisdiction to hear appeals throughout the US on specialized matters such as those involving patent laws, cases decided by the US Court of International Trade, and the US Court of Federal Claims.

Appeals from the 12 Circuit Courts of Appeals, appeals from the Court of Appeals for the Federal Circuit and appeals from the decisions of the State Supreme Courts dealing with federal law can be brought before the US Supreme Court, which is the highest court in the US.

Interestingly, the Supreme Court is not required to hear the case and the parties can file a "writ of certiorari" before the Supreme Court for conducting a hearing and if such writ is granted, the Supreme Court will conduct an oral hearing; otherwise, the decision of the lower court stands.

In most cases, therefore, the 12 Circuit Courts of Appeals are the final appellate courts.

1.5 Commercial Laws: Uniform Commercial Code and other Uniform Codes

Imagine this: you are the founder of a startup based in Delaware. However, you have suppliers for your products based in Wyoming and the majority of your customers are based in California. In such cases, if the state laws applicable to sales transactions or payments were different in all these three states, wouldn't it be difficult to arrive at the applicability of the law to such sales transactions?

1.5.1 Uniform Commercial Code

In view of this, the Uniform Law Commission together with the US Law Institute put together a comprehensive Uniform Commercial Code (UCC) and offered it to the states for their consideration.[6] All of the states adopted it within 20 years after Pennsylvania adopted it in 1953.

The Uniform Commercial Code deals with matters such as:

- Sale of goods - covering sales contracts, what can be considered "goods", termination and cancellation of sales contracts, rights and obligations of buyers and sellers, etc.

- Negotiable instruments such as promissory notes, checks, drafts, certificates of deposit, etc.

- Dealing between paying, collecting and intermediary banks and funds transfers

---

6. *Uniform Commercial Code,* Uniform Law Commission, https://www.uniformlaws. org/acts/ucc#:~:text=The%20Uniform%20Commercial%20Code%20 (UCC,the%20 interstate%20transaction%20of%20business.

- Letters of credit, warehouse receipts and bills of lading

- Manner in which ownership and interests in investment securities, whether certificated or uncertificated are recorded and transferred

- Manner in which secured transactions i.e. transactions for which a security of property is offered are recorded and disclosure of such transactions

- Leases of personal property

1.5.2 United States Code

In most countries, you will not find a single code for the compilation of laws on a specific matter.[7] However, the United States Code (USC) is exactly that. The USC contains codified laws on specific matters divided into 53 different titles. About half of these titles (27 of them) have been enacted into positive law. This means that the provisions in that title itself are the law on the subject. However, the other half are not laws by themselves, but rather a compilation of different laws on the subject. For example, Title 26 compiles the Internal Revenue Codes which have been enacted, but the title itself has not been enacted.

Unlike the UCC, which was offered by private institutions for adoption by each state, the USC contains federal-level matters and is applicable throughout the US.

---

7. *About the United States Code,* U.S. Government Information, https://www.govinfo.gov/app/collection/uscode/2020/title15

Besides the institution and functioning of the Congress and the President, the following are some of the important matters dealt with by the USC from a legal perspective:

- The Flag and Seal of the United States

- Agriculture

- Aliens and Nationality

- Arbitration

- Armed Forces

- Bankruptcy

- Banks and Banking

- Copyrights

- Crimes and Criminal Procedures

- Customs Duties

- Food and Drugs

- Foreign Relations and Intercourse

- Internal Revenue Code

- Judiciary and Judicial Procedure

- Patents

- Public Contracts

1.5.3 Individual State Codes

The individual states also have their own codes compiling the law on various matters, most of which are not dealt with by the USC. However, there can be some matters which can be covered by both the USC and state codes, such as matters relating to taxation and banking. This would mean that someone in that specific state would need to comply with both the USC and the state codes. For example, businesses would have to pay the federal tax according to the Internal Revenue Code and the state tax according to the relevant state code.

State codes can provide for the following:

- Businesses, Professions, and Occupations
- Business Organizations
- Municipalities
- Insurance
- Elections
- Education
- Health and Safety
- State Taxes
- Vehicles, etc.

 State codes are available easily on the relevant government, state codes, or statutes websites.

For example, the state codes for California can be found here: www.leginfo.legislature.ca.gov/faces/codes.xhtml

The state codes for Delaware can be found here: www.delcode.delaware.gov

The Statutes for Wyoming can be found here: www.wyoleg.gov/StateStatutes/StatutesDownload

The Statutes for Florida can be found here: www.leg.state.fl.us/statutes/

1.6 Are There Any Laws Relating to Ethics and Social Responsibility in the United States?

Generally, ethics are more a matter of practice than law. Though some practices follow the letter of law, they might not be ethical. However, certain categories of people in a society are required to hold and display a higher standard of conduct than others and thus, there are laws in place for conduct by such categories of people. Unethical behavior by such individuals thus becomes illegal too.

1.6.1 Laws relating to ethics applicable to government employees

The USC itself contains quite a few provisions that prohibit unethical conduct by government employees. In particular, Title 18 has quite a few provisions placing certain restrictions on government employees, which can be listed as under:

- Section 201 prohibits a public official from demanding, receiving, or accepting anything to commit an official act, or to violate official duty, or commit fraud. It equally prohibits bribing a public official.

- Section 203 prohibits any person who is an official or elected to become an official from accepting compensation in relation to any official matter while they hold such an office. It equally prohibits people from paying such compensation to an official.

- Section 205 prohibits officials from acting as an agent or attorney in cases where the US is involved as a party.

- Section 208 prohibits government officials from participating in acts where they or their family members have personal financial interests.

1.6.2 Laws relating to ethics applicable to specific professions

By virtue of different state laws, professionals such as accountants, medical practitioners, lawyers, etc. are regulated and not only unethical but also negligent conduct by such professionals is subject to disciplinary action.

For example, Section 455.227 of the 2021 Florida Statutes provides the grounds for discipline, penalties, etc. for professions and occupations and states that exercising influence on a patient or client for securing a financial gain by the professional or a third party is a ground for disciplinary action.[8]

1.6.3 Laws relating to ethics applicable to government in general

The Civil Rights Act of 1964 is an act which is considered to reflect the US government's commitment to bringing ethics into law by prohibiting discrimination in voting rights, use of public facilities, public education, employment, etc.[9]

---

8. *The 2022 Florida Statutes,* Website of the Florida State Legislature, http://www.leg.state.fl.us/statutes/index.cfm?App_mode=Display_Statute&Search_String=&URL=0400-0499/0455/Sections/0455.227.html

9. *Civil Rights Act, 1964, Milestone Documents,* National Archives of the United States Government, https://www.archives.gov/milestone-documents/civil-rights-act

1.6.4 Laws relating to ethics applicable to business organizations in general

Though people who are not subject to a professional license or who do not hold specific offices are not legally obligated to follow ethical behavior, where public money is at stake in a business, the people at the helm of such businesses can be subject to laws which require them to practice a certain standard of conduct and ethics.

For instance, Section 406 of the Sarbanes - Oxley Act of 2002 requires issuers of securities registered with the Securities and Exchange Commission to frame and disclose a code of ethics applicable to its principal executive, financial, and accounting officers who are collectively called "covered persons".[10] Such code of ethics is required to oblige the covered persons to act ethically in cases of conflict of interest, employ fair dealing with the company's customers and business partners, ensure appropriate compliance and disclosure, maintain confidentiality, and so on.

1.6.5 Laws mandating social responsibility for businesses

Though there are no specific laws mandating businesses to follow socially responsible practices in the US, this is a matter of self-regulation and large organizations do frame and implement codes and policies encouraging diversity, environment protection, appropriate health and safety policies, etc. Many organizations encourage their employees to be involved in giving back to society in the form of helping charity organizations, orphanages, etc. and conducting activities such as tree planting, educating children, and so on. A socially responsible company uplifts its image in the

---

10. *The Sarbanes-Oxley Act, 2002,* Website of U.S. Government Information, Page 45,
https://www.govinfo.gov/content/pkg/PLAW-107publ204/pdf/PLAW-107publ204.pdf
https://www.govinfo.gov/content/pkg/COMPS-1883/pdf/COMPS-1883.pdf

eyes of its employees, customers, and citizens in general and this is why organizations move towards such practices.

Quiz

---

1. The common law-based legal system originated in:

   a. Africa

   b. England

   c. US

   d. Japan

2. States do not get a fixed number of representatives in the House of Representatives because:

   a. this depends upon the constitution of each state

   b. the number is recalculated every ten years based on the population of the states

   c. each state has a different geographical area and the number varies based on changes in the area

   d. it depends upon how many representatives the state wishes to nominate each year

3. The US constitution provides for one Supreme Court, but the _____ has the power to establish inferior courts.

   a. President

   b. Congress

   c. Attorney General

   d. Secretary of State

4. **The highest trial courts are:**

    a. Intermediate Appellate Courts

    b. Circuit Courts

    c. District or Superior Courts

    d. Federal Claims Court

5. **The state of _____ is an exception in that it has a unicameral legislature.**

    a. Nevada

    b. Hawaii

    c. Nebraska

    d. Massachusetts

6. **Which of the following matters is not addressed by the Uniform Commercial Code?**

    a. Patents

    b. Sale of goods

    c. Leases of personal property

    d. Negotiable Instruments

7. **There are no specific laws relating to ethics relating to businesses in general, since:**

   a. businesses never follow ethics

   b. it is more a matter of self-regulation than imposition of law

   c. businesses have consistently opposed imposition of laws relating to ethics

   d. only professions are required to follow ethics, businesses are not required to do this

8. **An appeal from the decision of a District Court lies to:**

   a. the Court of Appeals for the Federal Circuit

   b. the Court of Appeals for the relevant Circuit

   c. the High Court for the District

   d. the Supreme Court of the US

9. **A state legislative bill is signed into law by the:**

   a. President

   b. Senator

   c. Governor

   d. Assembly member

10. The Uniform Commercial Code provides for _____

   a. how the laws in the US are enacted

   b. commercial relationships between the US and other countries

   c. commercial transactions such as sales, leases, etc.

   d. uniform prices for products

Answers	1 – b	2 – b	3 – b	4 – c	5 – c
	6 – a	7 – b	8 – b	9 – c	10 – c

Chapter Summary

◆ Most countries in the world follow legal systems based on civil law or common law. The US follows a common-law-based legal system.

◆ The US Constitution provides for the establishment of the legislature, executive, and judiciary functions and the manner in which laws are enacted in the US. The states have individual Constitutions of their own.

◆ District Courts or Superior Courts are the highest trial courts in a state and the Supreme Court of a state is the highest appellate court for that state. At a federal level, the highest appellate court is the Supreme Court of the US, though it hears matters very rarely, and thus in most cases, the 12 Circuit Courts of Appeals and the Court of Appeals for the Federal Circuit end up being the ultimate appellate courts.

◆ The United States Code is a compilation of nationally applicable laws, while the Uniform Commercial Code comprises laws on matters that the different states have adopted in their individual state codes.

◆ While there are no specific laws relating to ethics for people in general, there are laws demanding ethical conduct from the government, government employees, specific professions and occupations, and businesses where public money is involved.

Chapter 2

Forms of Business Organizations and How to Choose the Right Form

For a business, the choice of an appropriate form is a very important decision. Depending on the sector in which the business operates, the choice of the right form to carry on the business can significantly impact its growth and profitability. This chapter dwells on the different available forms of business in the US and factors that affect the choice of the right form.

Here is what you will know after reading this chapter:

- What are unregistered forms of businesses and what are their characteristics, advantages, and disadvantages?

- What are the registered forms of businesses available in the US and what are their characteristics, advantages, and disadvantages?

- What are the different forms of business which can be chosen by professionals?

- What are the factors you need to consider before you arrive at the right form for your business?

2.1 Unregistered Forms of Business: Sole Proprietorships and Partnerships

Let's assume there's someone named Sally Brown, who has a small business for designing brochures, pamphlets, etc. for businesses. She displays her work on her Facebook account and if someone reaches out to her to design something, she completes the design work for them on a freelance basis and gets paid for it.

This is known as a Sole Proprietorship. In a sole proprietorship, you are the business. The business does not have a separate existence from its owner. The owner does the work and gets paid for it. It does not matter if the business is carried out in the name of the sole proprietor or under a different name, often referred to as "doing business as" or "DBA". So if she carries on the business as "Sally Brown, Designer" or "Sally's Designs" or "Dashing Designs", it still does not separate the business from her, because irrespective of what you call it, the business needs her to do the work or for that matter, even to exist.

A common misconception is that if you file an application for a DBA with a local government, it means you have registered your business as a separate entity. A "DBA" application, also sometimes called a "Fictitious Name" application, only serves the purpose of informing the people that you are running the business under a specific name. To take our previous example forward, through a DBA filing, the people will come to know that "Dashing Designs" is actually being run by Sally Brown. It still continues to be a sole proprietorship, an unincorporated business form.

Many businesses are started as sole proprietorships. This is because starting a business as a sole proprietorship does not require many formalities to be fulfilled. If you are carrying on the business in your own name, you do not need to file even a DBA application.

Now let's assume Sally meets Mike, who is a video creator and editor and they decide that it might work out very well if they were to provide services to businesses together. They can then agree that they will call their business "Smashing Videos, Dashing Designs" and they will share whatever payments they receive from customers in equal amounts. This is a partnership in its simplest form. It is also known as a General Partnership. The business is still unregistered, and it cannot exist without its partners.

However, now, they can no longer carry on the business in any manner that they wish individually. They need to consult each other because half of the work is being done by each of them, so the decisions of the business should also be taken by them jointly. This is why the moment there is more than one person carrying on a business, there needs to be an "agreement" between them about who will do what work, who can take what decisions, who will bring how much money as capital for the business and how much share will each person get in the profits of the business. Maybe they will open a separate bank account which will be operated by both of them jointly.

Unlike sole proprietorships, partnerships are governed by law. Many state codes have provisions related to partnerships, even though these are not registered business forms. For example, Texas Statutes provide for creating a partnership agreement and what details it should not contain.[11]

In a partnership therefore, it is advisable, but not mandatory to sign an agreement between the partners describing how the partnership business will be managed. Partnerships are governed by state law, so one should check the laws of the state where the partnership will operate. Nevertheless, you still do not need to register the business with any government authority or regulator.

Sole proprietorships and partnerships, being unincorporated, do not require an income tax registration separate from the owners.

However, a huge limitation of these forms is that if you borrow money from someone in order to do the business and are not able to repay the loan, your personal property can be attached i.e. sold in order to repay such loans.

Following are some characteristics of unregistered businesses:

1. The business and the owner are the same, and hence the business can exist only as long as the owner exists.

2. The ownership and management of the business lie with the same person.

3. The owners are personally responsible for any debts that may be incurred by the business.

4. These businesses are relatively easy to start.

---

11. *Business Organisations Code,* Texas Statutes, Website of the Government of Texas, https://statutes.capitol.texas.gov/Docs/BO/htm/BO.152.htm

2.2 Registered or Incorporated Forms of Businesses

Incorporated businesses have an existence independent of their owners. Even if the owner dies, the business itself does not come to an end and can be carried on by its successors. Similarly, if the business borrows money, only the property owned by the business can be sold to recover the loan. The owner's personal property cannot be attached or sold.

However, this does not mean that you can simply incorporate a business and borrow money. Incorporated businesses require an investment of capital, which comes from the owners. For a lender to lend money, the business often has to show a track record of generating income and profits, and only then will a lender be convinced that the business can repay the loan.

While as a sole proprietor, you can simply maintain a list of your receipts and payments on an excel sheet, or just keep track of these through a bank account, in an incorporated business, you are required to prepare financial statements.

Let's look at the common forms of registered businesses available in the US:

2.2.1 Limited Partnerships

Each state has its own laws on limited partnerships. You will generally find these laws in the Business Organisations or the Corporations Code in the state codes or Statutes. The simple difference between a General Partnership and a limited partnership is that the liability of some partners in a limited partnership (known as limited partners) is limited to the amount of capital that they have contributed to the business.

However, limited partnerships still have a partner known as a General Partner (there can be more than one General Partner too), whose liability is unlimited i.e. if the limited partnership defaults on the repayment of a loan, the personal property of a General Partner can be sold in order to repay that loan.

General Partners are the people who run the business. Limited Partners are not involved in the day-to-day running of the business; their role is limited to contributing capital and receiving a share in the profits of the partnership.

In order to create a limited partnership, you need to file a certificate of limited partnership with the relevant Secretary of State. We will see how a limited partnership is formed in further detail in the next chapter.

Continuing our above example, let's assume that Sally and Mike need more money to buy laptops, design software, video software, etc. They have approached two of their friends who are willing to invest money in their business but have no idea how to design or work on videos. They are simply interested in investing the money and securing a profit share. Hence Sally and Mike create a limited partnership - Smashing & Dashing LLP and induct their friends as limited partners.

Sally and Mike carry on and expand the business with the help of the capital invested by their friends, and when the business turns profitable, everyone takes a share of the profits.

However, even with this form, the liability of Sally and Mike is still unlimited. In order to deal with this problem, Sally and Mike would need to create a Limited Liability Limited Partnership or an LLLP. In this form of limited partnership, the liability of all Partners is limited. However, the General Partners are still the ones actively carrying on the business and the Limited Partners invest the capital but are not involved in the day-to-day running of the business.

A limited partnership can enter into contracts in its own name and even if any of the partners of a limited partnership die, it can still continue to exist by inducting new partners.

Here are some features of a limited partnership:

1. The liability of limited partners is always limited to the extent of the amount contributed by them. In a Limited Liability limited partnership, the liability of General Partners is also limited.

2. A limited partnership can contract in its own name.

3. General Partners are involved in running the business of the Partnership. Limited Partners are not involved in the day-to-day functioning of the business.

4. A limited partnership is a registered form of business - it has an independent existence and can continue to exist even if any of the partners die.

2.2.2 Limited Liability Companies

Limited Liability Companies are hybrid forms of business that have some characteristics of both partnerships and corporations. This hybrid form is highly popular because of its dual features.

A Limited Liability Company (LLC) has the ease of formation of a limited partnership and the members of the LLC have limited liability too, similar to a limited partnership. However, unlike a limited partnership, the owner of an LLC can choose that the LLC shall be a manager-managed LLC i.e. the management will be separate from the owners. This feature of separation of ownership and management is not available in a limited partnership because the General Partners are owners. In a manager-managed LLC, it is not mandatory for the manager to be a member or to be given a profit share.

An LLC has an independent capacity to contract like a Corporation and as we noted, has the separation of ownership and management also, similar to a Corporation. However, unlike a Corporation, you cannot choose to have stock in an LLC and since the ownership cannot be divided into units of stocks, it is not easy to exit the membership of an LLC on a partial basis.

Also, while a Corporation has to pay separate federal income taxes and file separate returns, LLCs are not subject to separate federal income taxes, and while they would have to file separate tax returns if not treated as a "disregarded" entity, the income from the LLCs is "passed through" to the members and they can pay the taxes from the income of the LLC through their own returns.

State codes contain their own 'Limited Liability Company Acts' which regulate how LLCs can be formed, the compliance requirements, and other provisions.

Here are some of the features of a LLC:

1. The liability of the members of an LLC is limited to the extent of capital contributed by them.

2. The LLC has a separate existence from its members and can contract in its own name.

3. An LLC facilitates the separation of ownership from management i.e. the owners can choose that the LLC is managed by a manager who is not a member.

4. An LLC is not separate from the owner for the purpose of tax payments. The taxes are passed through to the owner.

2.2.3 Corporations

Corporations are the forms of business that have the highest degree of independence from the owner or owners. A corporation exists as a completely independent entity and is not impacted in any manner by the existence or otherwise of the owners. A Corporation can therefore contract in its own name, own properties, and also sue and be sued in its own name.

Corporations are managed by a Board of Directors and it is not necessary that any of the Directors hold any ownership in the corporation.

The ownership of a Corporation can be divided into a particular number of shares. It is, therefore, possible for someone to exit from the ownership of a corporation partially i.e. by selling some of the shares and retaining others.

Corporations are also taxed separately and are required to file tax returns of their own. Except for an S-Corporation, Corporations are subject to federal income taxes on their own profits.

Each state has its own 'Corporation Code' or 'Corporation Law' which provides for the incorporation, operation, and functioning of the Corporations. In general, Corporations are subject to a higher degree of record-keeping and compliance requirements than an LLC.

Corporations can further be divided into the following types:

C-Corporations

These are the default types of corporations. The Corporation Codes in the state Codes provide for the incorporation of these corporations. These types of corporations bear all the characteristics of the corporations noted above.

S-Corporations

S-Corporations are actually not separate types of corporations that can be incorporated. It is just an election of how a C-Corporation wants to be taxed. It is a flexible choice provided to the owners of a C-Corporation as to whether they want the corporation to be taxed as a "pass-through" entity. If such an election is made by filing the relevant form with the Internal Revenue Service (IRS), the Corporation is then considered to be an S-Corporation. However, there are certain conditions that need to be met if the owners of a C-Corporation wish to make this election. These are as follows:

1. The Corporation must have only individuals as its shareholders (except certain trusts and estates).

2. The Corporation must not have more than 100 shareholders.

3. The Corporation must have only one class of shares. Some Corporations have common stock and preferred stock. This is not possible in an S-Corporation.

4. Certain categories of corporations such as financial institutions are ineligible for electing to be taxed as an

S-Corporation. Hence, the corporation must not be in this category if the owners wish to make the election.

B-Corporations

Also known as Public Benefit Corporations (PBCs), this type is not available in all states. It is not a very popular form of business structure also, since it combines the for-profit nature of a business corporation with an intent to further some kind of public benefit, which is a difficult balance to maintain.

Unlike C-Corporations, B-Corporations tend to be more shareholder-driven than management-driven. The management is mandated to function not only in the best interests of the shareholders but also in a manner that furthers the public benefit envisaged in the certificate of incorporation of the B-Corporation.

Other than the public benefit aspect, B-Corporations are materially the same as C-Corporations. In 2021, few PBCs actually went public (had an initial public offering)![12]

2.3 Professions and the Forms of Business Used By Professionals

Professionals such as doctors or medical practitioners, lawyers, accountants, architects, etc. are required and expected to operate differently as compared to businesses. While businesses operate in a realm that is completely profit-driven, professionals are required to adhere to certain conditions in the license granted to

---

12. Christopher Marquis, *Public Benefit Corporations Flourish in the Public Markets,* Forbes.com, https://www.forbes.com/sites/christophermarquis/2021/06/14/public-benefit-corporations-flourish-in-the-public-markets/?sh=563da434233d

them while carrying on their business. They can form Professional Corporations (PCs) or Professional Limited Liability Corporations (PLLCs).

For example, if a businessperson influences a potential customer to make them buy more products, it isn't considered illegal. However, if a doctor were to do the same with a patient, the doctor may become subject to disciplinary proceedings under the law.

Most professionals practice under their own names or under the names of firms. For example, if you look at a list of the top law firms in New York by Chambers and Partners Ltd., you will discover that most of them are formed as Limited Liability Partnerships (LLPs).[13]

Many states which offer this type of business form do not permit certain licensed professionals to choose the LLC or Corporation form of business unless they choose one of these types.

From a taxation perspective, PCs can qualify for being taxed as a Personal Service Corporation (PSC) and secure some benefits in terms of taxation. In order to qualify as PSCs, PCs must be carrying on business in the fields of accounting, actuarial science, architecture, consulting, engineering, health (including veterinary services), law, and the performing arts.[14]

---

13. A Chambers law survey of *New York's top law firms in 2022,* Chambers-Associate. com https://www.chambers-associate.com/law-firms/new-yorks-top-law-firms

14. *Publication 542 (01/2022),* Website of the Internal Revenue Service, United States https://www.irs.gov/publications/p542#en_US_2022_publink100096247

Did you know?

California is a unique state in that it permits only licensed lawyers, accountants, and architects to form a Limited Liability Partnership.[15]

2.4 Factors Affecting the Choice of An Appropriate Business Form

Following are some factors which can be considered before someone chooses the right form of business for themselves:

1. **Separate existence from the owners (known as 'perpetual succession' in legal terms)**

   A founder needs to consider how dependent the business will be on his or her own skills. In our example of the designing business, the business will depend to a large extent on the skills of the designer. In such a case, the designer would either have to train other people or hire people who have the requisite skills in order to choose a form that would provide an independent existence. Therefore, in the beginning, such a business will usually be started as a sole proprietorship.

   If the business is such, as can be carried on without regard to the specific skill of a founder, for example, a business simply providing an e-commerce platform service, anyone can run it

---

15. *Limited liability limited partnership,* Website of the State of California Franchise Tax Board https://www.ftb.ca.gov/file/business/types/limited-liability-company/limited-liability-limited-partnership.html

once the website is in place. Therefore, it would be possible for such a business to exist without its founder being involved and the founder might choose to form it as an LLC right from the beginning.

2. Ease of formation

In the initial stages of a business, founders usually do not have either the time or the money to spend on complicated formation procedures. Most businesses, therefore, start out as sole proprietorships or at the most LLCs, if the other considerations weigh more.

3. Personal liability of the owners

This is a very relevant consideration, especially if the business sector is such that it is possible that there will be borrowing in significant amounts and also that the owner will be subject to a high degree of liability, for example, real estate. If a person is in the business of purchasing properties on a loan and renting them, the liability involved is high, and therefore, in such cases, founders will choose to form an LLC rather than functioning as a sole proprietor.

However, where personal liability considerations are rather low, like in our example of the business of a designer, the founder may choose to function as a sole proprietor.

4. Taxes

The way in which a business form is taxed is also very relevant to the choice of the appropriate form. In most cases, founders prefer that they do not have to file separate returns and that the entity is not taxed separately. However, where the income levels of an entity are high, it might even be advantageous for the founder to choose that the entity is taxed separately since in that case, the founder can control his or her own remuneration from the entity depending upon his or her individual tax situation.

For example, a corporation is taxed at a flat rate of 21% on a federal level. However, if the founder is earning well, the highest individual tax slab for 2022 is 37%. Therefore, the founder may choose to retain the income in the corporation and be subject only to a flat rate of 21%.[16]

5. Requirement for investment/borrowing

If the business is to be dependent upon a high degree of loans or investments from external parties, the preference of the lenders/investors will determine the choice of the appropriate form. For example, many private equity investors or angel investors prefer to invest in a C-Corporation since they can get preferred stock and an easier exit in the form of transfer or buyback of shares, or a public offering.

On the other hand, if a founder has significant personal assets, lenders might even prefer a sole proprietorship.

6. Record keeping, compliance and disclosures

A Sole proprietorship is subject to the least requirements in terms of record keeping, compliance and disclosures, while a Corporation is subject to the highest. Although this factor in

---

16. Sabrina Parys and Tina Orem, 2022-2023 *Tax Brackets and Federal Income Tax Rates,* nerdwallet.com, https://www.nerdwallet.com/article/taxes/federal-income-tax-brackets

itself does not usually drive the decision of a choice, it does have some weightage.

The most popular business form in the US is the LLC because of the flexibility, choice, and the mix and match features that it offers. This includes dividing the membership of an LLC into units.

Quiz

1. **Which form of business will a founder choose if he or she wishes that the ownership and management of the business are separate?**

   a. Sole proprietorship

   b. Partnership

   c. Limited Liability Partnership

   d. Corporation

2. **When a sole proprietor decides to convert the business to a partnership, he or she would need to:**

   a. register a separate entity for carrying on the business

   b. register as an S-Corporation

   c. enter into a partnership agreement to agree terms between partners

   d. make an application to mandatorily register a DBA

3. **Private investors often prefer a C-corporation as the chosen form of business because:**

   a. it is a pass-through entity

   b. they can include royalty and license payments through it

   c. they can get preferred stock which enables them to have special rights

   d. it does not permit shareholding by non-residents

4. **In a limited partnership, the liability of the limited partner is limited to the extent of:**

   a. the amount that they have invested in the business

   b. the amount that is allocated to them by the general partner

   c. the exact amount specified in the Limited Partnership Act of the relevant state

   d. the par value of the shares that they have been issued

5. **A Limited Liability Company is a hybrid between:**

   a. a proprietorship or partnership and a Corporation

   b. a proprietorship and a partnership

   c. a C-Corporation and an S-Corporation

   d. a partnership and a general partnership

6. **A PLLC is a:**

   a. Personal Limited Liability Company

   b. Professional Limited Liability Company

   c. Preemptive Limited Liability Company

   d. Private Limited Liability Company

7. **The difference between a C-Corporation and a B-Corporation is that B-Corporations are:**

   a. permitted to issue multiple classes of stock

   b. permitted to have non-resident shareholders

   c. more shareholder driven than management driven

   d. considered as disregarded entities

8. **Taxes are an important consideration in determining the form of business because:**

   a. each of the forms have different tax rates applicable to them

   b. whether or not you are required to file a separate return depends upon the form or business

   c. tax planning may be possible by structuring the business in the right form

   d. all of the above

9. **Which of the following is a condition required to be fulfilled for a corporation if it wishes to be taxed as an S-Corporation?**

   a. It should have at least 2 Directors

   b. It should have only one class of shares

   c. It should have a minimum of 50 shareholders

   d. It must be registered with the Securities and Exchange Commission

10. What does a "pass-through" entity mean?

    a. An entity in which all decisions are required to be passed through the board of directors

    b. An entity carried on by licensed professionals who have passed certain exams

    c. An entity in which the income is passed through to the owner

    d. An entity in which the resolutions are required to be passed through by the shareholders

Answers	1 – d	2 – c	3 – c	4 – a	5 – a
	6 – b	7 – c	8 – d	9 – b	10 – c

Chapter Summary

◆ Sole proprietorship and General Partnership are unregistered forms of business and therefore, their existence is not separate from their owners.

◆ Common forms of registered businesses available in the US include Limited Partnerships, limited liability companies, and corporations.

◆ Corporations can be C-Corporations, S-Corporations, and B-Corporations depending upon their choice of tax or purpose.

◆ Licensed professionals such as accountants, lawyers, or medical professionals can choose to operate as an LLP, PC, or PLLC.

◆ The choice of the form of business is dependent upon factors such as liability, taxation, preference of investors or lenders, etc.

This page is intentionally left blank

Chapter **3**

How to Form Business Entities and Leading States for Formation

A s we saw in the previous chapter, in order to register or incorporate business entities, there are certain formalities that are required to be fulfilled. Each of the state codes provides the requirements and procedures to form a business entity.

Key learning objectives of this chapter include the reader's understanding of the following:

- Which are the states which are preferred the most for forming limited partnerships, limited liability companies, and limited partnerships?

- What are the roles of the Secretaries of State in the formation of business entities?

- How are Limited Liability Companies formed?

- How are limited partnerships formed?

- What is the procedure to incorporate a business corporation?

3.1 States Which Are Preferred For Registration or Incorporation of Entities

There are certain states which are preferred by businesses as a base for incorporation because of various reasons. If you see most lists of the best state to incorporate a business entity in,[17] Delaware and Wyoming top most of the lists because of certain benefits that these states offer.[18] In particular, Delaware is a favorite for establishing corporations in the US, even by non-resident founders. Delaware registered a whopping 249,427 new business entities in the year 2020.[19] As of 2020, 68% of the Fortune 500 entities were registered in Delaware.

Wyoming is a favorite state for registering LLCs. The first quarter of 2022 saw 26,312 domestic entities being registered in Wyoming, with LLCs being formed in the highest number.[20]

---

17. Hannah Collymore and Randolph Vialva, *Best State to Form an LLC in 2023*, bizreport.com, https://www.bizreport.com/llc-by-state/best-state-for-llc-formation

18. *Top 3 Best States to Start and Incorporate a Business*, legalnature.com, https://www.legalnature.com/guides/top-3-best-states-to-start-and-incorporate-a-business

19. *2020 Annual Report Statistics*, Delaware Division of Corporation, https://corpfiles.delaware.gov/Annual-Reports/Division-of-Corporations-2020-Annual-Report.pdf

20. Statistics for Domestic entity charters filed with the Secretary of State for Wyoming, Website of the Secretary of State for Wyoming, https://sos.wyo.gov/Business/docs/22Q1Domestic.pdf

Here are some reasons why Delaware is preferred as a state for registering corporations:

1. It is harder to find out information about the owners of a Delaware corporation. Unlike some other states, it is not possible to download information about a corporation and its owners free of charge, and even upon payment, you get to see only limited information. It thus allows owners to hold ownership of a Delaware corporation anonymously.

2. It is one of the most preferred states for receiving funding. Investors, incubators, and accelerators prefer their investee entities to be registered in Delaware because of its clear and business friendly corporation laws.

3. The Court of Chancery in Delaware, which hears thousands of cases dealing with commercial matters of corporations registered in Delaware, works with principles of equitable justice, where there are no remedies in law.[21] This is particularly favorable for commercial and contractual matters.

4. The formalities for establishing an entity in Delaware are quite simple and facilitate easy incorporation even by non-residents.

5. The state also offers extremely fast processing, including processing within an hour, on the payment of expedited processing fees.

6. The annual formalities for a Delaware corporation are not cumbersome and expensive. If an entity is not doing business, which can be the case in the initial years for a

---

21. William T. Quillen and Michael Hanrahan, *A Short History of the Court of Chancery*, The Widener University School of Law, https://courts.delaware.gov/chancery/history.aspx

startup, the annual cost of maintaining the entity is around $450, including the franchise tax.[22]

Here are some reasons why Wyoming is preferred as a state for registering Limited Liability Companies (LLCs):

1. Wyoming does not have any personal income taxes, meaning you will simply be liable for your federal income tax if you incorporate in Wyoming. The annual license fee is $60 or 0.0002 per dollar of the value of the Company's assets located and employed in Wyoming, whichever is greater.[23] Compare that with the likes of California, which charges a minimum of $800 as the annual franchise fee on an LLC.[24]

2. Similar to Delaware, it's very difficult to extract information about the ownership of a Wyoming LLC because these states protect the privacy of information.

3. Wyoming is a hotbed for crypto companies.[25] It was the first state to add a DAO (Designated Autonomous Organization) supplement in its Limited Liability Company Act, providing a legal entity to house such a business in.[26]

22. *Kaviya A, 10 Advantages of Incorporating Your Company in Delaware, USA,* vakilsearch. com, https://vakilsearch.com/blog/10-advantages-of-incorporating-your-company-in-delaware-usa/

23. *Filing Fee Schedule of the Wyoming Secretary of State,* Website of the Wyoming Secretary of State, https://sos.wyo.gov/Business/docs/BusinessFees.pdf

24. *Limited Liability Company,* Guidance by the State of California Franchise Tax Board, Website of the State of California Franchise Tax Board, https://www.ftb.ca.gov/file/business/types/limited-liability-company/index.html

25. Chris Matthews, *How Wyoming became the promised land for bitcoin investors,* marketwatch.com, https://www.marketwatch.com/story/how-wyoming-became-the-promised-land-for-bitcoin-investors-11619201182

26. Troutman Pepper, *Wyoming Amends DAO Legislation Enabling DAOs to Dictate Quorum Threshold on an Individual Basis,* jdsupra.com, https://www.jdsupra.com/legalnews/wyoming-amends-dao-legislation-enabling-2457236/#:~:text=On%20March%209%2C%20Wyoming%20amended,Wyoming's%20Limited%20Liability%20Company%20Act.

3.2 What is the Role of the Secretary of State in the Formation of Companies?

The Secretaries of State are constitutional officials. The Constitutions of different states provide for the appointment or election of the Secretaries of State.

For example, Section 10, Article III of the Constitution of Delaware provides that the Governor will appoint the Secretary of State who will hold the office until the pleasure of the Governor.[27]

Article 4, Section 11 of the Wyoming Constitution provides that the Secretary of State is an elected official holding office for a term of 4 years.

In most states, the duties of the Secretaries of State include the following:

1. Registering different types of entities such as Limited Liability Companies, Corporations, Limited Partnerships, and Statutory Trusts, etc.

2. Serving as an office for filing annual reports and amendments by the entities and providing certified copies

3. Providing apostille and authentication certificates

4. Maintaining records and minutes of proceedings of the legislature

5. Maintaining the filing and records of Uniform Commercial Code Documents

---

27. *Article III of the Delaware Constitution,* Website of the Government of Delaware, https://delcode.delaware.gov/constitution/constitution-04.html#P370_48625

Therefore, for the formation, recording changes or amendments in the certificates/articles of formation/incorporation/organization, annual report filings and also for closing down or dissolving the entities, the Secretaries of State are the relevant office to be contacted in all cases.

In the case of most states, the guidance and procedure for the formation, ad-hoc filings, and annual filings are clearly provided on the websites of the Secretaries of State.

3.3 How Are Limited Liability Companies Formed?

Each state has its own Limited Liability Company Act and the procedure and provisions for the formation of LLCs are provided in that statute. Therefore, the procedure for the formation of a Limited Liability Company will differ from state to state. However, some basic requirements such as the requirement to file an initial certificate or articles containing the details of the person registering the entity and the details of the registered agent are similar across many states.

We can take a look at how a LLC is formed in the most favored state as we noted above, Wyoming. The provisions contained in the Wyoming Limited Liability Company Act - Title 17 Chapter 29 of the Wyoming Statutes govern the formation and operation of Limited Liability Companies in Wyoming. Article 2 governs the formation of the Limited Liability Companies.[28]

---

28. 2022 *Wyoming Statutes,* Website of the Government of Wyoming, https://wyoleg. gov/NXT/gateway.dll?f=templates&fn=default.htm

Article 2 provides that Limited Liability Companies can be formed by an organizer and the organizer is required to file a document called the Articles of organization with the Wyoming Secretary of State, which is required to contain the following information and documents:

1. The name of the Limited Liability Company (LLC)

2. The address of the registered office of the LLC

3. The name of the initial registered agent at the registered office

4. A consent for appointment by the registered agent

The website of the Wyoming Secretary of State enables filing the Articles of Organization online.[29]

The LLC is formed when the Articles of Organization become effective. There are many formation agents providing LLC formation services for as low as $50.

3.4 How to Incorporate Business Corporations?

Just like the LLCs, the states' codes also provide for the establishment of Corporations. Therefore, the procedures for incorporation of a Corporation are also different in different states. However, here too, similar to LLCs, the requirement for providing the details of the person incorporating the entity and the details of the registered agent is similar across many states.

---

29. *Forms and Publications,* Website of the Wyoming Secretary of State, https://sos.wyo. gov/forms/default.aspx?root=Business

For Corporations also, let us look at the procedure for incorporation of a Corporation in Delaware, and this can give us a general idea of the procedure for incorporation. Title 8, Chapter 1 lays down the Delaware General Corporation Law. Subchapter 1 provides information for the formation of a corporation.

1. The first step that needs to be taken is to check if the intended name of the entity is available. This can be done on the website of the Delaware Secretary of state itself.

2. In order to form a Delaware Corporation, the second step that needs to be taken is to appoint a registered agent who will accept the service of process for the corporation in the state.

3. Thereafter, a certificate of incorporation needs to be filed with the Secretary of State containing the name and address of the incorporator, the name and address of the registered agent, and the amount of capital with which the corporation is to be formed. There can be further details included such as the names of the directors of the corporation if the intention is to name them in the certificate of incorporation.

4. Once the Secretary of State takes the certificate of incorporation on record, they will send a filed copy of the certificate back to the address of the incorporator. This confirms that the Corporation is incorporated.

5. Once incorporated, the incorporator is required to elect the board of directors of the Corporation in order to adopt the by-laws, appoint the officers of the corporation, and issue the initial shares.

3.5 How Are Limited Partnerships Formed?

Interestingly, unlike LLCs and Corporations, in the case of limited partnerships, there is some uniformity in the laws of the states, because a majority of the states have adopted the Uniform Limited Partnership Act of 1976. As of June 2022, 26 states have adopted the Revised Uniform Limited Partnerships Act of 2001.[30]

Based on the Uniform Limited Partnership Act, in order to form a limited partnership, a certificate of limited partnership must be delivered to the Secretary of State, containing the following information:

1. The name of the limited partnership

2. The street and mailing address of the partnership's principal office

3. The name, street, and mailing address of the partnership's registered agent in the state

4. The name, street, and mailing address of each General Partner

5. A statement as to whether the partnership is a limited liability limited partnership

The partnership is formed when the certificate of limited partnership becomes effective, at least two people have become partners, at least one person has become a general partner, and at least one person has become a limited partner.

---

30. *Limited Partnership Act,* Revised, Website of the Uniform Laws Commission, https://www.uniformlaws.org/committees/community-home?CommunityKey=d9036976-6c90-4951-ba81-1046c90da035

Quiz

1. **In which of the following states is the Court of Chancery located?**

   a. Massachusetts

   b. Nevada

   c. Delaware

   d. Wyoming

2. **Investors prefer their investee entities to be located in Delaware because of:**

   a. its zero personal tax rates

   b. its low franchise tax rates

   c. its zero federal corporate income tax rate

   d. its clear and business friendly laws

3. **In order to form a limited partnership, you need to file a:**

   a. Certificate of incorporation

   b. Certificate of Limited Partnership

   c. Articles of Incorporation

   d. Certificate of formation

4. The first step required to form a corporation is to:

   a. file the articles of organization

   b. submit the certificate of formation to the Secretary of State

   c. search if the name of the corporation to be incorporated is available

   d. apply for an Employer Identification Number with the IRS

5. The person who forms a LLC in Wyoming is called:

   a. an incorporator

   b. an organizer

   c. a director

   d. a registered agent

6. In order to form an LLC in Wyoming, where are the articles of organization required to be filed?

   a. With the Internal Revenue Service

   b. With the Wyoming Secretary of State

   c. With the Wyoming Registrar of Trademarks

   d. With the Securities and Exchange Commission

7. **Which of the following is not mandatorily required to be included in a certificate of incorporation for a Delaware entity?**

   a. Name and address of the registered agent

   b. The amount of authorized capital

   c. Name and residential address of the Directors of the Corporation

   d. Name and address of the incorporator

8. **Which of the following is not a duty of the Secretaries of States?**

   a. registering different entities

   b. registering copyrights for businesses

   c. providing apostilles and authentication services

   d. serving as office for filing annual reports by entities

9. **Which of the following actions of the Delaware Secretary of State confirms that a corporation is incorporated?**

   a. The Secretary of State will send an email to the incorporator informing of the incorporation

   b. The Secretary of State will send a filed copy of the certificate of incorporation

   c. The Secretary of State will issue a certificate of good standing to the corporation

   d. The Secretary of State will send the articles of incorporation to the incorporator

10. Which of the following documents provides for the appointment of the Secretaries of States?

   a. The Constitution of the relevant state

   b. The Constitution of the US

   c. The Uniform Commercial Code

   d. The US Revised Statutes

Answers	1 – c	2 – d	3 – b	4 – c	5 – b
	6 – b	7 – c	8 – b	9 – b	10 – b

Chapter Summary

◆ Delaware and Wyoming are preferred states for the formation of corporations and LLCs because of their favorable privacy and tax regime.

◆ The formalities related to the formation or incorporation of entities are to be carried out before the Secretaries of State in each state. The appointment, powers, and duties of the Secretaries of States are provided for in the Constitutions of each state.

◆ Forming an LLC or Corporation involves the appointment of a registered agent and the filing of a certificate or articles of formation or incorporation with the relevant Secretary of State.

◆ The procedure for forming a limited partnership is more uniform across the states because it is provided for in the Uniform Limited Partnerships Act which has been adopted by many states.

Chapter **4**

Basic Taxation Regime and Tax Registrations Required

Before starting any business, one of the most important considerations for a founder is to know what taxes a business will be subject to. This is because knowing the tax obligations of the business, based on its specific form can help a founder make an informed decision about the right kind of business form to choose.

Here is what we will learn in this chapter:

- What is the difference between direct and indirect taxes and which type of direct and indirect taxes are prevalent in the US?

- Which types of taxes are imposed at a federal level?

- Which types of taxes are imposed at a state level?

- What are the different types of registrations required for businesses under the tax laws in the US?

4.1 Difference Between Direct and Indirect Taxes

Direct taxes are the taxes that are to be borne by the person on whom these are levied, such as income tax and estate tax. These taxes must be paid by the person who earns the income and the person who receives an estate in inheritance, respectively. It cannot be passed on to someone else.

On the other hand, indirect taxes are those taxes that are passed on to someone else. For example, sales tax can be levied on the trader who is selling some products, but this tax will be passed on by the trader to the customer who buys the products. If you see the invoice for the sale, you will notice that it includes the price of the products purchased and additionally, there will be sales tax added to it as well as the total price. The trader will collect the tax from the customer and deposit it with the government.

4.2 Direct Taxes Prevalent in the United States

In the US, the Internal Revenue Code (Title 26 of the United States Code) governs the levy of federal income tax, estate and gift taxes, employment taxes, and certain excise-related taxes at a federal level.[31]

---

31. *Tax Code, Regulations and Official Guidance,* Website of the Internal Revenue Service, United States, https://www.irs.gov/privacy-disclosure/tax-code-regulations-and-official-guidance

Following are the main types of direct taxes that are prevalent in the US:

4.2.1 Individual and Corporate Income Tax

Income tax is levied under the provisions of Section 61 of the Internal Revenue Code, which provides the definition of 'Gross Income'.[32] This simply means that income from all the sources listed in this definition will be considered for the purposes of determining how much income tax a taxpayer will pay. This list includes income from any kind of services rendered: income from a business, income interest, rents, royalties, dividends, annuities, pensions, share of partnership, etc. We must note that this is an inclusive definition. This means that if you are receiving income from any other sources, it will still be included within the income to be considered for taxation purposes.

That, however, does not mean that the tax rate will simply be applied to one's total income received from all activities. There are certain deductions allowed from the gross income, so you can arrive at income on which the tax rates will be applied. This is known as taxable income.[33]

The tax rates are also applied differently based on the different levels of income. These are known as tax slabs or tax brackets. The lowest tax rate for the tax year 2022 was 10% for a single person's income of $10,275 and the highest rate was 37% for a single

32. *26 U.S. Code S 61, Gross income, defined,* Cornell Law School Legal Information Institute, https://www.law.cornell.edu/uscode/text/26/61

33. *26 U.S. Code S 63, Taxable Income, defined,* Cornell Law School Legal Information Institute https://www.law.cornell.edu/uscode/text/26/63

person's income if it's greater than \$539,900.[34] In order to figure out how much tax you have to pay, you would need to find out your taxable income and find out the bracket within which it falls.

The income tax rate is calculated differently for an entity. It is applied directly on the profits earned by a corporation. For a corporation, the flat federal tax rate for the year 2022 was 21%, which had remained unchanged from the previous year, 2021. This means that irrespective of whatever the company earns, it would have to pay a tax of 21% on its profits.

4.2.2 Capital Gains Tax

Capital gains tax is levied when you earn profit from selling your property. If you have held the property for more than a year, the profit is known as a long-term capital gain and if you have held it for less than a year, it is known as a short-term capital gain. Capital gains taxes are levied at a federal level at the rate of 15% if your taxable income is higher than \$40,400 as an individual and \$80,800 for married couples who file their returns jointly.[35]

4.2.3 Kiddie Tax

In the absence of the "Kiddie Tax", parents could file separate tax returns for their children and since the income of the children would be lower, there would be lower tax rates applicable to the child. Thus, parents could simply gift their investments to

---

34. *Tax inflation adjustments for the year 2022,* Website of the Internal Revenue Service, United States, https://www.irs.gov/newsroom/irs-provides-tax-inflation-adjustments-for-tax-year-2022

35. *Topic No. 409, Capital Gains and Losses,* Tax Topics, Website of the Internal Revenue Service, United States, https://www.irs.gov/taxtopics/tc409#:~:text=Capital%20Gain%20Tax%20Rates,or%20qualifying%20widow(er).

their children so that the children will receive the interests and dividends and such income will be taxed at lower rates instead of the higher rate applicable to parents.

In order to plug this loophole, the "Kiddie Tax" was imposed to tax the "unearned" income of children. This applies to passive income like interests or dividends. This would not apply in case the child is actually earning the income - for example, income earned by child actors.

For the tax year 2022, if a child has unearned income over $2,200, there would be a specific tax applied on such income.[36]

4.2.4 Estate Tax

This tax is applicable on the value of the property that is passed on as an inheritance. Although it will ultimately be paid by an heir from the estate received in inheritance, the tax is applied on the person who passes on the inheritance for their right to transfer their estate. In most cases, this tax will not be paid because it is only payable if the fair market value of the property is in excess of $12.06 million.[37] Therefore, it would apply only to the heirs of affluent families who receive a large estate in inheritance.

---

36. *Topic No. 553, Tax on a Child's Investment and Other Unearned Income,* Tax Topics, Website of the Internal Revenue Service, United States, https://www.irs.gov/taxtopics/tc553

37. *Guidance on Estate Tax,* Website of the Internal Revenue Service, United States, https://www.irs.gov/businesses/small-businesses-self-employed/estate-tax

4.2.5 Gift Tax

The exemption limit for estate tax i.e. $12.06 million counts as the total limit for giving gifts too![38] However, in case of gifts, for the year 2022, there was also an annual limit of $16000 per individual. Only gifts to individuals are subject to tax, and any amount or benefit that you give to someone without expecting anything in return can be classified as a gift. Interest-free loans can also be classified as gifts.

You would become subject to the payment of a "tax" in very rare circumstances because your gifts in excess of the annual limit would be adjusted against the limit of how much you can give someone in the form of an estate.[39] However, you would have to file a gift tax return if you exceed the annual limit for an individual.

There are also exclusions available. For example, a gift to your spouse is not considered within the list of taxable gifts. If you want to avoid the hassle of filing a gift tax return, you must ensure that the gift is either an exclusion from taxable gifts or is below the annual limit.

4.2.6 Employment Taxes

If you are employed, you will often notice that the amount of salary that was on your offer letter and the amount that you receive in your bank account are different. This is because your employer is required to withhold (keep back) the amount of taxes

---

38. *Frequently Asked Questions on Gift Taxes,* Website of the Internal Revenue Service, United States, https://www.irs.gov/businesses/small-businesses-self-employed/frequently-asked-questions-on-gift-taxes

39. Tina Orem and Sabrina Parys, *Gift Tax: How it Works, Who Pays, and Rates,* nerdwallet.com, https://www.nerdwallet.com/article/taxes/gift-tax-rate

payable by you from your salary and deposit these on your behalf with the government. This means that you will receive your salary only after the tax has been deducted from it.

Since this is a duty cast on the employers, if you are running a business, it is your duty to withhold the following taxes from the payments that you make to the employees:

1. Income tax

2. Social Security tax

3. Medicare tax

4. Federal unemployment tax (also known as FUTA)

The Income tax that you deduct from your employee's salary will be based on the total income of the employee and any information provided by the employee related to the deductions they can avail. For the year 2022, the Social Security taxes were deducted at the rate of 6.2% from the salary and the employer is required to add a further 6.2% from their own pocket and deposit a total of 12.4% with the government. For the year 2022, the Medicare taxes were deducted at the rate of 1.45% from the salary, and the employer was required to add a further 1.45% from their own pocket and deposit a total of 2.9% with the government.

Businesses are required to deduct the Federal Unemployment Tax (FUTA) in 2022 if they paid wages of more than $1500 in any calendar quarter in the years 2021 or 2022 or if the business had employees for at least some days or part days in 20 different weeks in the years 2021 or 2022.[40] Most businesses would be covered under these requirements. The FUTA tax rate is 6% on the first $7000 that is paid to each employee. If you have paid

---

40. Publication 15, *(Circular E), Employer's Tax Guide,* Department of Treasury, Internal Revenue Service, https://www.irs.gov/pub/irs-pdf/p15.pdf

your state unemployment taxes in full, you may be able to claim a deduction from the payment at the federal level.

4.2.7 Property Tax

Property taxes are levied and paid at the state and local levels and different taxes can have different methodologies for calculating the tax rates. For example, while California taxes properties at each county level, on the basis of creating different Tax Rate Areas (TRAs),[41] New York taxes properties based on the classes of properties.[42] Washington on the other hand taxes properties at county level based on the different Tax Code Areas (TCAs).[43] The rates of taxes also vary depending on the relevant state and you can find these by either visiting the state government website or the website of the relevant county where the property is located. All 50 states levy property taxes.

4.3 Indirect Taxes Prevalent in the United States

In most countries, if you travel, you will find that when you purchase something, there is a value-added tax (VAT) applied on the price of the products, which you can claim back when you are leaving the country. Interestingly, there is no VAT in the US. The primary indirect taxes are sales tax and excise tax.

---

41. *Tax Rate Area Lookup - Auditor-Controller of the Los Angeles County,* Website of the Government of Los Angeles County, https://auditor.lacounty.gov/tax-rate-area-lookup/

42. *Property Tax Rates,* NYC Department of Finance Website of the City of New York, https://www1.nyc.gov/site/finance/taxes/property-tax-rates.page

43. *Guidance on How to Calculate Property Tax,* Website of the San Juan County, Washington, https://www.sanjuanco.com/1392/How-to-Calculate-Property-Tax

4.3.1 Sales and Use Taxes

Sales taxes are not applied at a federal level, but rather the different states have their own rates for a statewide sales tax. The states may also have different rates of sales tax applicable for specific items. Sales taxes are applied on sales, rentals, storage services, or payment for admission to something, such as a fair or an event.

For example, in Florida, the statewide sales tax is 6%, but in the case of the sale of electricity, the rate is 6.95%.[44]

Use taxes are applied when someone buys a taxable item for self-consumption and does not pay sales tax. For example, if you have bought a product with the intention to resell it, but instead you use it for your own personal use, you would have to pay a use tax on it.

4.3.2 Excise Taxes

Excise taxes are applicable at a federal level on the manufacture, retail, or even consumption of certain specific products. For example, taxes are imposed on certain chemicals and chemical products, coal mining, kerosene used in aviation, sports wagering, use of heavy highway vehicles, etc.

The rates of excise taxes vary depending on the product and are applied to the value of manufacture or consumption of the specific product. The proceeds from these taxes are also applied for different purposes. For example, the excise tax collected on

---

44. *Florida Sales and Use Tax,* Website of the Florida Department of Revenue, https://floridarevenue.com/taxes/taxesfees/Pages/sales_tax.aspx#:~:text=Florida's%20general%20state%20sales%20tax,of%20commercial%20real%20property%20%2D%205.5%25

coal mining is deposited in the Black Lung Disability Trust Fund, which is used to benefit workers in the coal mines who may contract the black lung disease.

4.4 Which Types of Taxes Are Imposed at a Federal Level?

The major taxes which are applied at the federal level are income tax, corporation tax, and employment taxes. The other taxes applicable at the federal level which we saw above such as estate taxes, excise tax, etc. contribute relatively less to the federal revenue compared to the three types of taxes discussed above.

Most taxes that are applied at the federal level are direct taxes.

4.5 Which Types of Taxes Are Imposed at a State Level?

While most taxes imposed at a state level are indirect taxes, there are some direct taxes imposed at the state level too.

4.5.1 State Income Taxes and Corporate Taxes

Most states impose income taxes on the incomes of the residents of the states. Although some states such as Wyoming, Nevada, Florida, Texas, and Washington do not levy personal income taxes.

State personal income tax rates can vary and some states have high income tax rates such as California which has the personal income tax rates ranging from 1% to 13.3%, Hawaii which has personal income tax rates ranging from 1.4% to 11% and New Jersey, which has personal income tax rates ranging from 1.4% to 10.75%. Not only individuals, but corporates are also subject to taxes at the state level in the ranges of 2% to 11%.

Being aware of the tax rates in different states can enable the decision about the state in which a business entity should be formed. Absence of personal income taxes is why businesses prefer to form LLCs in Wyoming, since as we noted before, an LLC is a pass-through entity.

4.5.2 Franchise Tax

Some states collect a tax on the businesses formed in that state known as the "Franchise Tax". Although it is called a tax, it is actually a charge by the state to enable businesses to take the benefits of the infrastructure or favorable opportunities in that state. For example, Delaware charges a minimum franchise tax of $175 on a Delaware corporation,[45] while California charges a franchise tax of $800 on corporations formed and conducting business in California.[46] This tax is payable on an annual basis.

---

45. *Guidance on Franchise Taxes,* Division of Revenue, Website of the Government of Delaware, https://revenue.delaware.gov/business-tax-forms/franchise-taxes/#:~:text=The%20minimum%20tax%20is%20%24175.00,a%20maximum%20tax%20of%20%24200.000.

46. *Guidance on Corporations,* Website of the State of California Franchise Tax Board, https://www.ftb.ca.gov/file/business/types/corporations/index.html

4.5.3 Sales and Use Taxes

We already noted above how states charge sales taxes and use taxes on products sold/consumed within the state.

4.5.4 Property Taxes

We already noted above how states charge property taxes depending upon the tax rate areas or property classes.

4.5.5 Other Taxes

Other taxes can be levied by state governments and the taxes can depend upon the government's intentions to discourage the use of some products, like the so-called "sin" taxes on cigarettes or vape products, alcohol, or gambling activities.

States can also levy taxes on gas, inheritance, gifts, over-the-counter drugs, travel, etc. depending upon the state budget.

4.6 What Are the Important Registrations Required for Businesses Under the Tax Laws in the United States?

4.6.1 Employer Identification Number (EIN)

Technically, a business is only required to secure an employer identification number if it will be hiring employees and depositing employment taxes as we discussed above.[47] However, a business bank account cannot be opened in the US for an entity until you have an EIN and therefore, it is important to secure one by making an application to the Internal Revenue Service (IRS).

The application for an EIN can be made online if the business owner has a Social Security Number (SSN) or an Income Tax Identification Number (ITIN).[48] If not, the application can be made by phone or by fax in form SS-4. It is a very simple form that requires only the details of the business to be filled in. If your principal business is outside the US, you can even apply for an EIN by phone.

4.6.2 Sales Tax Permit

In order to charge and deposit sales tax with the state governments, traders who sell taxable goods are required to register for a sales tax permit. These registrations can usually be completed online, with only basic business-related information to be provided by the person looking to register.

---

47. *Guidance on how to Apply for an Employer Identification Number (EIN) Online,* Website of the Internal Revenue Service, https://www.irs.gov/businesses/small-businesses-self-employed/apply-for-an-employer-identification-number-ein-online

48. *Guidance on how to Apply for an Employer Identification Number (EIN),* Website of the Internal Revenue Service, https://www.irs.gov/businesses/small-businesses-self-employed/how-to-apply-for-an-ein

Below are some state government websites to reach if you are looking to register for a sales tax permit in these states:

California: https://onlineservices.cdtfa.ca.gov/

New York: https://www.tax.ny.gov/bus/st/register.htm

Washington: https://secure.dor.wa.gov/home/Login

Nevada: https://www.nevadatax.nv.gov/#

Wyoming: https://excise-wyifs.wy.gov/

Florida: https://taxapps.floridarevenue.com/taxregistration

Texas: https://comptroller.texas.gov/taxes/permit

Quiz

1. Which of the following is an indirect tax?

    a. Capital gains tax

    b. Estate tax

    c. Sales tax

    d. Corporate tax

2. Wunderland LLC is an entertainment company. It has 10 employees. Which of the following will it definitely be required to pay?

    a. Property tax

    b. Capital gains tax

    c. Social security tax

    d. Insurance tax

3. Gloria is working as a coder with Infotrek Inc. Which of the following taxes will she be required to pay?

    a. Capital gains tax

    b. Software tax

    c. Sales tax

    d. Income tax

4. Emma, an 8 year old girl, owns stocks that are gifted by her parents. She receives a good amount of dividend from the stocks. Her parents are required to pay a tax on her dividend income. This is an example of:

   a. Direct tax

   b. Indirect tax

   c. Hybrid tax

   d. Pass-through tax

5. Who is required to pay the estate tax?

   a. The liquidator of the estate

   b. The attorney making the will

   c. The heir who receives the estate

   d. The spouse of the deceased person

6. Who is required to pay the gift tax?

   a. The person giving the gift

   b. The person receiving the gift

   c. The person to whom the gifted property is sold

   d. The trustee

7. **Which of the following is an exclusion for the gift tax for the year 2022?**

   a. Gifts to mother

   b. Gifts to spouse

   c. Gifts to father

   d. Gifts to government employees

8. **Which of the following taxes can be paid on the basis of a "Taxable Rate Area"?**

   a. State sales tax

   b. Property tax

   c. Capital gains tax

   d. Estate tax

9. **On what amount is a use tax required to be paid?**

   a. Fair market value property given on rent

   b. Fair market value of all products used

   c. Fair market value of products used on which sales tax has not been paid

   d. Amount payable for use of government property such as parks

10. **Which of the following taxes levied on coal mining are deposited toward the Black Lung Disability Trust Fund?**

    a. Employment taxes

    b. Sales taxes

    c. Excise taxes

    d. Corporate taxes

Answers	1 – c	2 – c	3 – d	4 – a	5 – c
	6 – a	7 – b	8 – b	9 – c	10 – c

Chapter Summary

◆ Direct taxes are those taxes which are borne by the person on whom they are levied, while indirect taxes are those taxes which are passed on by the person on whom they are levied to another person.

◆ The direct taxes prevalent in the US are income taxes, corporate taxes, employment taxes, capital gains taxes, estate taxes, and property taxes. Indirect taxes prevalent in the US are mainly sales taxes and excise taxes. There is no VAT in the US.

◆ Income taxes, corporate taxes, and capital gains taxes are charged at both the federal and state level. Sales taxes and property taxes are only charged at the state level, and states can charge multiple other types of taxes depending upon the state budget and the intention to encourage or discourage the use of certain products.

◆ Two important registrations required to be secured by the businesses are the registration to secure an Employer Identification Number (EIN) at the federal level and to register for a Sales Tax Permit at the state level. Both applications can be made online and by regular mail.

This page is intentionally left blank

Chapter **5**

Employment Law, Social Security, and Other Benefits Systems

As we noted in the previous chapters, businesses can start from a sole proprietorship and then grow gradually to become large corporations. Initially, a founder would be working alone to develop the business and also to make the product or provide the service. But as the business grows, it is not possible for a founder to do everything by himself or herself and therefore, they would need to hire people to work for them.

Good businesses will follow practices that encourage employees to work in an encouraging environment where employees can also learn and grow and get better returns for the extra efforts put in by them.

However, there may be businesses that can take undue advantage of employees also. In order to avoid this, most countries have laws to ensure that businesses do not exploit people whom they hire. All businesses would have to follow such laws.

In this chapter, we will learn about:

- Which are the different types of employment laws prevalent in the US?

- What does the Equal Employment Employment Opportunity Commission do?

- How can businesses in the US hire foreign workers?

- What are the laws prevalent in the US relating to social security?

- What are the different types of employment incentive schemes which are used by businesses in the US?

5.1 An Overview of the Employment Laws in the United States

In the US, the employment laws are administered by the United States Department of Labour,[49] which has set up various agencies under it, in order to look after specific areas related to labor laws. In addition, each state has its own labor and employment laws and they enforce those laws.

49. Website of the U.S. Department of Labor https://www.dol.gov/

The employment laws in the US can be mainly divided into the following broad categories:

- Laws relating to wages and remuneration

- Laws relating to health and safety

- Laws relating to leaves

- Laws relating to unions

- Laws relating to other employment conditions such as protection against discrimination

- Laws relating to workers in specific industries such as agriculture, mining, construction, transportation, etc.[50]

5.1.1 Laws relating to wages and remuneration

These laws include the following:

- Fair Labour Standards Act, which provides for the payment of the minimum wages and payment overtime at the rate of one and a half times the regular rate of pay.[51] As of July 2022, the federal minimum wage rate is $7.25 and overtime is payable for hours worked after 40 hours worked in the week. This law is administered by the Wage and Hour Division which enforces the laws relating to wages in the US.

- Laws relating to workers' compensation programs prevalent at the federal and state levels such as

---

50. *Summary of the Major Laws of the Department of Labor,* Website of the Department of Labor, https://www.dol.gov/general/aboutdol/majorlaws

51. *Wages and the Fair Labor Standards Act,* Wage and Hour Division, https://www.dol.gov/agencies/whd/flsa

- Federal Employees Compensation Act providing for compensation in the case of death or disability of federal employees in certain circumstances

- Longshore and Harbor Workers Compensation Act which provides for compensation and medical care to certain maritime employees

- The Energy Employees Occupational Illness Compensation Program Act providing for certain benefits to certain employees, contractors, and subcontractors

5.1.2 Laws relating to health and safety

The main US federal law relating to the health and safety of the employees is the Occupational Safety and Health Act (OSHA), which mandates employers to provide to the employees a place of employment which is free from recognized hazards which are likely to cause death or serious physical harm to the employees.[52] It is administered by the Occupational Safety and Health Administration. Under the scheme of the OSHA, various standards are established for various industries generally or for specific industries such as construction, maritime, and agriculture for the purpose of maintaining the health and safety of the employees.

5.1.3 Laws relating to leave

The federal law relating to leave is the Family and Medical Leaves Act which requires employers to give the workers up to

---

52. *Occupational Safety and Health Act, 1970,* Website of the United States Department of Labor, https://www.osha.gov/laws-regs/oshact/completeoshact

12 weeks of unpaid leave, with the protection of the job for the purpose of childbirth or serious illness of employee, spouse, child or parent.[53] Several states, including New York and California, have additional family leave statutes that grant additional family leave.

5.1.4 Laws relating to unions

The federal law relating to unions is the Labor-Management Reporting and Disclosure Act.[54] It provides for the democracy and proper management of the unions by requiring the union officials, employers, and labor consultants to file certain reports and laying down standards for the election of the union officials.

5.1.5 Laws relating to protection against discrimination

The US has an extensive legal framework of laws against discrimination. The federal laws against discrimination can be listed as under:

- Title VII of the Civil Rights Act of 1964, which makes it illegal to discriminate against someone on the basis of race, color, religion, national origin, or sex and also makes it punishable to retaliate against someone who lodges a complaint against discrimination

- The Pregnancy Discrimination Act which makes it illegal to discriminate against women because they are pregnant or on account of pregnancy-related conditions

---

53. *Family and Medical Leave Act,* Website of the United States Department of Labor, https://www.dol.gov/agencies/whd/fmla

54. https://www.dol.gov/agencies/olms/laws

- The Equal Pay Act which provides for equal pay for equal work i.e. that men and women should be paid the same wages for the same work

- Title I of the USs with Disabilities Act which makes it illegal to discriminate against disabled people

- The Genetic Information Nondiscrimination Act of 2008 which makes it illegal to discriminate against employees or applicants because of their genetic information

- Sections 501 and 505 of the Rehabilitation Act which make it illegal to discriminate against a person with a disability or to retaliate against someone who has lodged a complaint against discrimination [55]

5.1.6 Laws relating to workers in specific industries

Certain sectors that may have a higher threat to the health and safety of an employee than usual. For example, workers in the construction and transportation industries can be more prone to accidents. This is why it is necessary that there are specific laws relating to such workers. Some of such laws which relate to workers in specific industries are:

- Migrant and Seasonal Agricultural Worker Protection Act which provides for regulating agricultural employers or people who hire migrant and seasonal agricultural workers.[56] The provisions relate to wages, safety standards, and other benefits for such workers.

---

55. *Laws Enforced by Equal Employment Opportunity Commission,* Website of the Equal Employment Opportunity Commission, https://www.eeoc.gov/statutes/laws-enforced-eeoc

56. *Migrant and Seasonal Agricultural Worker Protection Act,* Website of the U.S. Department of Labor, https://www.dol.gov/agencies/whd/agriculture/mspa

- The Federal Mine Safety and Health Act provides for the health and safety of the mine workers, provision of training to the mine workers, and enables inspectors to close dangerous mines.[57] There are also prescribed penalties for violation by the mining businesses.

- Although there is no specific act for construction workers, the OSHA provides for specific health and safety standards to be followed by businesses hiring construction workers.

- Similar to construction, OSHA also provides for specific health and safety standards for maritime employees. Further, the Longshore and Harbor Workers Compensation Act requires employers to provide for the funding of compensation for the workers.

5.2 Discrimination and the Role of the Equal Employment Opportunity Commission

As we noted above, the US has many laws which prohibit discrimination in employment on various grounds such as race, age, sex, color, religion, pregnancy, disability, or genetic information. Discriminating between employees or even job applicants on the basis of these factors can lead to serious consequences and it adversely affects the reputation of the employer also.

However, it is not enough that there are laws in place to ensure protection against discrimination. These laws also have to be enforced. In order to ensure that these federal laws are

---

57. *Federal Mine Safety and Health Act,* Mine Safety and Health Administration, U.S. Department of Labor, https://arlweb.msha.gov/REGS/ACT/ACTTC.htm

implemented and enforced, an oversight body known as the Equal Employment Opportunity Commission (EEOC) has been established.[58]

The EEOC has the power to investigate cases of discrimination by employers who are covered by the laws. Most employers who employ at least 15 employees are covered by the applicable laws. This indicates that even entities that are in very early stages of growth cannot discriminate between their employees.

If, after an investigation, the EEOC believes that there is a possibility that an employer has applied discrimination in hiring, remuneration, working conditions or wages, etc., it can initiate a process of conciliation between the person who filed the charge and the employer. In some cases, the EEOC may have the right to file a suit in the public interest, however, this is rare.

5.3 Laws Relating to Hiring Foreign Workers

Governments generally enable hiring foreign workers where there is a shortage of skilled labor in a specific area. For example, for a long period of time, the profession of nurses has been in short supply in multiple countries and therefore, someone who is a qualified nurse would have a very good chance of securing a visa to work in a foreign country. Similarly, there can be skilled workers in different professions such as engineering, information technology, accounting, etc. which can be in short supply and therefore, professionals in these professions can secure employment visas.

---

58. Migrant and Seasonal Agricultural Worker Protection Act, Website of the U.S. Department of Labor, https://www.dol.gov/agencies/whd/agriculture/mspa

The Immigration and Nationality Act is covered in Title 8 of the United States Code and provides for different types of employment visas for employment of foreign nationals in specialty occupations.[59] The most common visa is the H1-B visa which provides for the temporary employment of foreign workers in specialty occupations such as IT, finance, medicine, mathematics, science, etc.

The visas need to be obtained by foreign workers prior to starting work in the US if they are seeking work in the US. In the event that a US business is looking to hire foreign workers, the business would have to prove to the Department of Labor that there is actually a scarcity of workers in that profession and enough workers are not available at that specific wage rate. For this purpose, the employer would have to first obtain a certification from the Department of Labor and then petition the US Citizen and Immigration Services for a visa to sponsor the foreign worker.

Currently, however, it is possible for a US business to hire a foreign worker easily for specific project-based assignments through various remote working platforms. This way, the temporary worker can complete the work without having to travel to the US and US businesses can have access to foreign labor without having to follow immigration-related processes.

---

59. *Immigration and Nationality Act,* Website of the U.S. Citizenship and Immigration Services https://www.uscis.gov/laws-and-policy/legislation/immigration-and-nationality-act

5.4 Laws Relating to Social Security

One of the main laws relating to any payments for social security in the US is the Employee Retirement Income Security Act (ERISA).[60] ERISA provides for establishment of plans related to retirement and health for the benefit of the employees.

The key provisions of the Act are:

- It sets minimum standards for participation, vesting, benefit accrual, and funding for the participants in the plan.

- Fiduciary responsibilities are attached to the persons authorized to control and manage the assets belonging to the plan.

- It provides for a grievance redressal mechanism so that the participants can avail complete benefit of the plans.

- Participants have the right to sue in case of breach and to go for higher appeals in case of any non-compliance by those who are supposed to manage the plans in their fiduciary capacity.

- A federally chartered corporation called the "Pension Benefit Guaranty Corporation" (PBGC) is formed in order to guarantee payment of certain benefits to the participants in the event of any defined benefit plan being terminated.

- ERISA does not cover the plans maintained outside the US primarily for the benefit of nonresident aliens or unfunded excess benefit plans.

---

60. *Employee Retirement Income Security Act,* Employee Benefits Security Administration, U.S. Department of Labor, https://www.dol.gov/agencies/ebsa/laws-and-regulations/laws/erisa

- There are provisions for compliance assistance whereby publications and other relevant materials are provided to assist the employers and other bodies that work for employee benefit plans, for better compliance with ERISA plans.

5.5 Employee Incentive Schemes and How These Are Used By Companies

As we discussed right at the beginning of this chapter, good businesses incentivize their employees when the employees perform well. Businesses can use various methods to provide incentives to their employees for two reasons:

- To reward them for their performance

- To encourage them to perform even better the next time

Incentives can be provided directly in the form of additional money, such as a bonus or a profit share. However, there are also methods to incentivize employees with means other than money, such as stock options or restricted stock units. These are known as equity-based incentives. Let's discuss each of these and their benefits and limitations.

5.5.1 Bonus

Bonus is the most common method of incentivizing employees. Every year, businesses rate the performance of their employees by their agreed rating methods and where the employees have done well, they are rewarded with a bonus. Often, bonuses are based on the performance of the business as well, even if the ratings of the employees continue to be the same as the previous year. Therefore, if the business has earned more profits in a year, it may distribute bonuses to its employees.

The good thing about a bonus is that the employees directly get the money which they can spend. However, a bonus also means that the employee will have to pay an increased amount of tax in that year. The other limitation is that it does not ensure retention. It is possible that an employee can resign very soon after being paid a bonus.

5.5.2 Profit Share

This is a better method than a bonus because it makes an employee feel like they are sharing the profits of the business and therefore, it encourages the employees to work towards earning a higher profit for the next year so that they get a better profit share.

It is also a more scientific method since the profit shares are calculated based on the contribution of the specific department to the business and in turn, the employee's contribution to the department.

For example, the amount of the profit is considered to be 100%, and then the sales, products, and operations departments may be given a higher weightage for a share of profit than the legal department, since these departments directly contribute to the profits, whereas the legal department is a cost function. If the sales department is given 35% weightage, for instance, there will be further weightage given for performance by the Head of Sales, telecallers, etc. and the profit will be shared accordingly.

But, the problem with this method is that it can be very difficult to decide the weightage of the respective departments and employees and some departments may feel like they are treated on a lesser footing than their colleagues. In this method also, the employee receives the money directly, so there will be higher tax implications.

5.5.3 Employee Stock Options

Employee stock option plans (ESOPs) are an equity-based method of incentivizing the employees. In this method, the employee does not receive any money directly. However, they are given something called "options", which they can use at a later date to buy the shares of the company at a discounted price.

Often in the case of startups, the value of the shares increases very fast because the company is growing at a very fast rate. This is why ESOPs can become a very attractive method of incentivization. When a startup is acquired or if it comes out with an Initial Public Offering (IPO), the employees would be able to sell the shares received by them either to the acquirer or through a broker in the case of an IPO. If the business has been growing fast, the employees can get multifold returns for the shares offered to them.

The benefit of the ESOPs is that under ESOP plans, shares are granted over a period of time and not all at once. This becomes a strong incentive for someone to continue being employed with the business. Employees also feel like they are part owners of the company when they get the shares.

The limitations of an ESOP are that if the employees are not able to sell the shares - either to an acquirer or through an IPO, they begin to feel like they have not been given any incentive at all. Also, once an employee becomes a shareholder, they also get voting rights in the company, which may not be something that the management prefers.

5.5.4 Restricted Stock Units

Restricted Stock Units (RSUs) are also spread over a period of time, just like the ESOPs, but RSUs can be settled for cash and shares. This means that instead of buying shares from the company like ESOPs, employees can just be allotted shares or provided cash for the difference in the value of the shares when they were granted the RSU and the value when the RSUs are settled

Like ESOPs, RSUs provide a benefit only when they "vest." Vesting happens when you get the right to get shares for the RSUs.

Here is an example:

Let's consider that Sam was granted 400 RSUs by his company so these vest equally over a period of four years. This means that Sam gets the right to get shares for 100 RSUs each year. After a year, when Sam gets rights for 100 RSUs, if the value of the shares is $20, Sam gets the rights to get shares worth $2000 (100 RSUs x $20). However, the company will deduct some amount for taxes and allot shares to Sam for the balance amount. Alternatively, the company can simply give Sam $2000 minus taxes in cash.

The benefit of RSUs is that the employee does not have to "purchase" the shares like an ESOP plan. They are simply granted the shares. The limitation, however, is that the employees may still not get access to the money until those shares are actually sold.

Quiz

1. **Which of the following laws provides for minimum wages?**

   a. The Wages and Equal Remuneration Act

   b. The Fair Labour Standards Act

   c. The Employee Retirement and Income Security Act

   d. The Workers Compensation Act

2. **The OSHA mandates employers to:**

   a. provide a place of employment which is free from recognized hazards

   b. make a doctor available on premises of employment

   c. provide for regular health checks of the workers

   d. provide for safety railings around the factory premises

3. **The standard overtime rate as provided for by the Fair Labour Standards Act is:**

   a. one and half times the standard rate of pay

   b. twice the standard rate of pay

   c. thrice the standard rate of pay

   d. same as the standard rate of pay

4. **The laws relating to wages and compensation of workers are administered by the:**

    a. Wages and Compensation Department

    b. Equal Employment Opportunity Commission

    c. Wage and Hour Division

    d. Wages and Income Security Board

5. **The Equal Employment Opportunity Commission has the powers to:**

    a. conduct raids on establishments based on information

    b. require various organizations to implement a diversity policy

    c. introduce reservation in various industries for employment of minority representatives

    d. investigate the charges of discrimination against employees

6. **In order to hire foreign workers, US businesses have to prove to the Department of Labour that:**

    a. they have sufficient funds to pay salaries to the foreign workers

    b. there is scarcity of appropriate skilled workers

    c. they are primarily owned by foreigners

    d. they have an agreement in place with the foreign worker being hired

7. The H1-B visa is for the purpose of:

   a. permanent employment of foreign workers in a management capacity

   b. hiring of workers specifically from India

   c. temporary employment of foreign workers in specialty occupations

   d. hiring of workers specifically from Australia

8. The ERISA is a law relating to:

   a. provision of health and safety to the workers

   b. establishment of plans related to retirement and health of the employees

   c. provision of employee stock options to the employees

   d. compensation of federal government employees

9. Which of the following is an example of an equity-linked incentive scheme?

   a. Festival bonus

   b. Profit sharing

   c. Restricted stock units

   d. Commission on extra sales

10. A limitation of ESOPs is that:

a. employees may not be able to sell the shares easily

b. employees get the shares all at once

c. ESOPs are only given to senior management

d. ESOPs are optional to be taken by the employees

Answers	1 – b	2 – a	3 – a	4 – c	5 – d
	6 – b	7 – c	8 – b	9 – c	10 – a

Chapter Summary

◆ The legal framework for labor laws in the US consists of laws relating to wages and remuneration, laws for health and safety of the employees, laws for protection against discrimination, and laws relating to workers in a specific industry.

◆ The US has extensive laws relating to prohibition of discrimination on various grounds such as age, sex, religion, color, genetic information, etc. The Equal Employment Opportunity Commission (EEOC) administers these laws.

◆ In order for businesses in the US to hire foreign workers, they need to secure certification from the Department of labor and prove to it that there is a scarcity of the required skill in the US and that the workers are not available for appropriate wages.

◆ The Employee Retirement Income Security Act (ERISA) provides for the establishment of appropriate plans relating to retirement and health for the benefit of the workers.

◆ Various incentive schemes for the workers prevalent in the US can include schemes that provide monetary incentives such as bonuses and profit-sharing and equity-linked schemes such as employee stock options and restricted stock units.

This page is intentionally left blank

Chapter 6

Contract Law and Enforcement of Contracts

A business exists to earn profits. Profits can only be earned when there are transactions - such as buying and selling products, providing services in exchange for money, taking a loan, making an investment, etc.

Unless you are buying something directly off the counter, almost all transactions require that there are some terms and conditions attached to them - for example, that the products to be provided by a seller must be of a certain quality, or that the payment for the products must be made by the buyer within two days of delivery. Even if you buy something off the counter, there are certain terms and conditions.

In the case of long-term or ongoing transactions, these conditions can be put into documents known as "contracts".

Key learning objectives of this chapter include the reader's understanding of the following:

- What are the essential elements in order to make a contract valid?

- What are the different types of contracts which are provided for in the UCC?

- What are the different types of contracts covered under common law in the US?

- Can contracts be entered into by an electronic mode?

- What are the contract law provisions in relation to payments for goods and services in the US?

- Which laws govern the banking system and electronic financial transactions and how can these impact contracts?

- What happens when a party breaches a contract? How are contracts enforced?

6.1 Essential Elements of a Valid Contract

There are a few things that need to be present in order for a contract to be considered a valid contract. If any of these elements are missing, the contract will not be enforceable, which means that even if someone does not perform their obligations under the contract, the other person will not be able to do anything about it.

6.1.1 Consensus ad idem

In order for a contract to materialize, it is essential that both the people involved in the transaction agree to the terms and conditions. If one of them does not agree, the deal does not happen. Therefore, in order for a valid contract to happen, there needs to be *"consensus ad idem"* or consensus on an idea. For example, if you are looking to purchase a phone, the seller should be willing to sell you the phone and both of you would also have to agree on the price. Unless you are willing to buy and the seller is willing to sell for the same price, there is no consensus.

6.1.2 Offer and acceptance

For a consensus to be reached, someone has to make an offer and the other person has to accept that offer. Read the following conversation happening in a gift shop:

"How much does that figurine cost?" (This is an invitation to offer)
"$35." (This is an offer)
"Okay. Please pack it." (This is acceptance)

As against this, read the below conversation:

"How much does 1 kg of onions cost?" (This is an invitation to offer)
"$3." (This is an offer)
"Can you sell it for $2.50?" (This is a counter offer)
"Okay. You can take it." (This is acceptance)

As you can see, unless there is an offer and an acceptance, the deal does not get completed. In business contracts also, similar to the shop front, there can be a lot of negotiations before an offer gets accepted, and the terms may be around a lot of other things than just the price.

6.1.3 Capacity to contract

Business contracts, which are intended to be enforced, are different from social agreements. Your friend calling you with an offer to watch a movie together and you accepting it can be called a social agreement. However, someone commissioning a company to shoot a film is a business contract. Business contracts have monetary implications and can result in loss of money if not performed.

Since such contracts have monetary implications, it is important that the people who are contracting have the maturity and mental capacity to understand the implications of their actions before they enter into a contract. This is why there is a requirement that a person must be of legal age (18 years in most states) and of a sound mind in order to enter into an enforceable contract.

Someone who is in an aberrated state of mind on account of consuming alcohol or drugs may not be considered to be of a sound mind and hence, may not be considered to have the capacity to contract.

6.1.4 Legality

As regards to the legality of a contract, there are two different things to be considered:

● The object or the purpose of the contract must be legal

- There must be an intention to create a legally binding relationship

As an example, you cannot contract with someone to rob a bank. It's a contract with an illegal purpose. As regards to the intention, both parties must have an intention to enforce the contract if the other party fails to perform their obligations. As an example, if a father lends a certain amount of money to his son, and does not intend to make the son repay the loan if he cannot, then this is not a contract created with the intention of making it legally binding. If however, a bank lends money to its client, the intention is to make the client repay or have his or her assets sold if they cannot repay. Here, there will be an intention to create a legally binding relationship.

6.1.5 Consideration

In a contract, there must be something known as a "quid pro quo" or a "give and take". In legal language, this is known as consideration. Unless there is a consideration involved for either party i.e. both the parties are getting something out of the contract, it will not be valid. Hence if someone is just making a donation, this will not be considered a contract because they will not get anything in return. On the other hand, if the contract relates to selling certain products, there will be consideration involved for both parties, because one party will receive the products and another will receive the price of the products.

6.2 Contracts Provided for in the Uniform Commercial Code

The UCC deals with contracts relating to goods, primarily sales and leases of goods.[61] Basically, it provides for contracts which deal with products which are a) tangible and b) movable.

Hence, it does not deal with contracts relating to things that are not tangible, like services or intellectual property. It also does not deal with contracts relating to things that are immovable, for example, land or a house or an apartment.

The two main types of contracts which the UCC deals with are sales and leases. Let's remember that sales contracts or lease contracts are also contracts and therefore, all the essentials of a valid contract as we discussed above need to be present for these contracts also. However, there are some interesting requirements for these contracts that are provided for in the UCC, which we can take a look at.

6.2.1 Sales contracts[62]

Sales contracts are the most common contracts. Consider how many items you purchase on a daily basis. In order to make these products available to you at the shop level or the department store level, the shop owner or the department store owner has to purchase these products in bulk either from a wholesaler or the manufacturer of the product. Hence, while the purchase you

---

61. *Uniform Commercial Code,* Cornell Law School, https://www.law.cornell.edu/ucc

62. *Uniform Commercial Code, Article 2 - Sales,* Cornell Law School, https://www.law. cornell.edu/ucc/2

make may be of a small amount, the purchases from a wholesaler or manufacturer would be of very large amounts. It is therefore important to understand how the law applies to these contracts. We will discuss a few interesting elements of a sales contract that the UCC provides for.

1. **Implied warranty of merchantability:** When you buy a specific product, you generally assume that the product is fit for the purpose that you are buying it for. For example, if you buy a pen, you assume that it will be able to write, otherwise, what use is a pen that cannot write? This is why the law provides that a "merchant" must sell a product that is "merchantable" i.e. which serves the purpose that it is generally intended for, even if the buyer has not made such a specific request. Hence, food items must be edible, pens must be able to write, and clocks must show time.

2. **Passing of title in goods:** If you are out to buy a product, when does it become yours? After you make a payment and get physical possession of it, right? However, consider this - you may have purchased something on Amazon and paid for it in advance before it is delivered to you. In this case, it becomes yours upon the payment even if you have not received it physically yet. The UCC, therefore, provides that the "title" or the ownership of the goods cannot pass from the seller to the buyer until the goods are identified as being part of the contract. Once the goods are identified, the title will pass depending upon what is agreed between the buyer and the seller.

3. **Seller's remedies:** The UCC provides for the remedies available to the seller in case the buyer does not accept the goods or does not pay the price or in general, does not keep up to his part of the contract. Among other remedies, the

seller can withhold the delivery of the goods and also claim damages for the breach of contract.

4. **Buyer's remedies:** The UCC also provides for the remedies available to the buyer in the event that the seller fails to deliver the goods.

6.2.2 Lease contracts[63]

As against sales, in a lease transaction, the lessor only allows the use of a product to the lessee, and the ownership of the product does not pass from one person to another.

Difference between a lease and secured transactions is that in the case of a lease, the lessee only gets possession of the product and pays a lease rental for the use. However, at the end of the lease period, the leased product has to be handed back. In the case of a secured transaction, the ownership of the product has already passed and the product will be taken back by the lender only if the borrower does not pay for it.

For example, if you hire a costume, you would have to return it after you have used it and you would pay for using it for a short time. On the other hand, if you buy a car on a hire purchase, the ownership of the car passes to you when you buy it. You have to repay the loan, but you would not have to give back the car at the end of the hire purchase period.

---

63 *Uniform Commercial Code Article 2A, Leases,* Cornell Law School, https://www.law. cornell.edu/ucc/2A.

6.3 Contracts Provided for Under Common Law in the United States

6.3.1 Contracts for services

As against contracts that provide for the sale of goods, multiple contracts provide for the delivery of services in return for a payment, such as painting a house, making a film, etc. However, the principles of merchantability and change of title cannot apply in this case. Hence in the case of these contracts, there needs to be a lot of things described in the contract such as how the work needs to be done, by when it needs to be done, whether the payment is to be based on milestones, etc. The way these contracts are interpreted is therefore based on common law i.e. how judges have decided cases related to similar contracts.

6.3.2 Contracts for intellectual property

In the case of these contracts, though services are not provided, intangible property is transferred. For example, a developer may create a specific type of software program for a company. In this case, it is actually the program that the company is buying, not the services of the developer. However, it is not something that someone can hold in their hands and therefore, it is not governed by the UCC. It will be governed by the legislation for the specific intellectual property. In the case of software, a copyright on the software is the relevant intellectual property and the transfer of such intellectual property will be governed by copyright laws.

6.3.3 Contracts for immovable property

Contracts for real estate like land and buildings are governed by common law and since real estate deals are heavily influenced by the different regions and practices in a specific state, these tend to be interpreted based on case law in the specific state. For example, the property types, prices, and terms prevailing in California are likely to be very different from those prevalent in New Jersey and therefore, the decisions of the appellate courts of the relevant circuit will be more relevant for interpreting contracts in those states.

6.4 E-contracts

The pandemic situations prevalent in 2020 and 2021 made it necessary for people to find ways of executing contracts over the internet. Contracts were entered into over the internet, services were delivered over the internet and payments too, were made over the internet. In the US, there are two main laws that impact the execution and implementation of electronic contracts.

6.4.1 Electronic Signatures in Global and National Commerce Act (ESIGN)[64]

This Act provides that contracts that are of an interstate or foreign nature are permitted to be entered into in an electronic mode and contracts entered into electronically would be as valid legally as paper contracts.

---

64. *Electronic Signatures in Global and National Commerce Act,* U.S. Government Information Website https://www.govinfo.gov/content/pkg/PLAW-106publ229/pdf/PLAW-106publ229.pdf

However, where institutions want consumers to agree to the terms of a contract electronically, there are certain specific provisions that they need to take care of:

- Firstly, they need to inform consumers that they have an option of requesting the contract in a physical form, whether the consent provided by the consumer applies to a single transaction or multiple transactions, etc.

- The consumer must also be provided with the information about the hardware and software required for accessing the information properly and the procedure or method to access the information properly before the consumer consents as a part of an electronic contract.

6.4.2 Uniform Electronic Transactions Act (UETA)[65]

With the exception of New York and Puerto Rico, at the end of July 2022, all the states adopted the UETA. The UETA provides for the following main things:

- The contract will be signed electronically only if both parties intend that the contract should be signed electronically.

- Organizations that are engaged in online businesses and ask for the customer's consent to a transaction electronically are required to provide the customers with a copy of the UETA consumer consent disclosure, through which the customers will agree to use an electronic document to carry out their transactions. Furthermore, customers must also be informed about the process to withdraw their consent and

---

65. *Electronic Transactions Act,* Uniform Laws Commission, https://www.uniformlaws. org/committees/community-home?CommunityKey=2c04b76c-2b7d-4399-977e-d5876ba7e034

the business will be required to ensure that the customer has not withdrawn their consent.

- The system that is used to create the contract should not only be able to attach the consent to a specific contract, but also maintain a record of such consent.

6.5 Contract Law Provisions Related to Payments

6.5.1 Negotiable instruments

Negotiable instruments are covered under Article 3 of the UCC.[66] According to the UCC, there must be the following four characteristics of a negotiable instrument:

- It must be signed by the maker or the drawer

- It must relate to a specific amount of money

- It must either order the payment of money or contain a promise to pay

- It must be payable on demand or within a definite period of time

Types of negotiable instruments are drafts and notes. Drafts are instruments that contain an order for a payment to be made on demand. On the other hand, notes are instruments that contain a promise to pay at a certain later date. For example, a check is a

---

66. *Uniform Commercial Code, Article 3,* Negotiable Instruments Act, Cornell Law School, https://www.law.cornell.edu/ucc/3

draft - it can order the payment to be made on demand. On the other hand, a certificate of deposit is in the nature of a promissory note, which promises that the payment shall be made at a later date.

6.5.2 Electronic Payments[67]

Section 4A of the UCC provides for electronic payments; basically, it relates to fund transfer or wire transfers from one bank account to another. In the case of electronic fund transfer, the person making the payment is known as the "originator" and the person to whom the funds are being transferred is called the "beneficiary".

It may be possible that the funds are not directly transferred from the originator's bank to the beneficiary's bank account and that these have to be routed through an intermediary bank. This is especially true in cases where the currency in which the originator's bank account is held is different from the currency in which the beneficiary's bank account is held.

When an electronic fund transfer is made, an acceptance of the payment is considered to have been completed on the earlier of the following three dates:

- When the beneficiary's bank receives the fund

- When the beneficiary's bank makes the fund available to the beneficiary

- The opening of the bank on the next business day following the date when the beneficiary's bank receives a payment

---

67. Uniform Commercial Code, Article 4A, Cornell Law School https://www.law. cornell.edu/ucc/4A

order from the sending bank for facilitating the payment to the recipient.

6.6 Impact of Laws Relating to Banking Systems and Electronic Financial Transactions on Contracts

Electronic payments are made not only by fund transfers but also by credit cards and debit cards.

In addition to the UCC, a Federal Reserve Regulation known as Regulation Z governs the use of credit cards including liability for payment, unauthorized use, disclosures, and non-payment and billing dispute resolution.[68] In addition to Regulation Z, the Electronic Fund Transfers Act governs the use of debit cards and transfers and a system of transferring payments known as ACH transfers which enable making deposits by businesses in order to enable administering their payrolls.

Laws relating to payments are very important because clauses relating to payments included in the contracts provide for the mode in which the payment for the goods or services will be made. Furthermore, depending on the method of payment chosen, the payment for a contract is considered to have been completed on a specific date. This would help to determine whether the obligation in relation to making the payment was completed within time or if it was a breach of contract which may lead to damages becoming payable for breach.

---

68. *Electronic Funds Transfers and Other Payment Systems*, LawShelf Educational Media, https://lawshelf.com/videocoursesmoduleview/electronic-funds-transfers-and-other-payment-systems-module-4-of-6

6.7 Breach and Enforcement of Contracts

We already discussed the court system prevalent in the US in Chapter 1 of the book. Let's think of a little example of why you would like to initiate a court proceeding. Assume that you provided services to a company for designing their brochures and after getting the work done, the company did not pay you.

This is known as a breach of contract because the company defaulted upon its obligations of making the payment to you. A good contract would in itself provide for the consequences of its breach. For example in the above case, you might have provided for in the contract that for every week of delay in the payment, the company will be responsible to pay a penalty of a certain amount of dollars.

However, if this is not resolved based on the provisions of the contract, parties may have to invoke the court system in order to enforce the contracts. [69]The party which complained about the breach may be able to get the following remedies for the breach of contract:

1. **Specific performance:** This means that the court will ask a party to do what they have not done. For example, if a seller has not delivered the products, the court will ask the seller to deliver the products. If a party has not made the payment of the initial amount or the penalty, the court will ask it to make such payment by way of a judgment.

---

69. Content team of Miller Law and review by Marc Newman, *6 Common Remedies for Breach of Contract in Business*, Miller Law, https://millerlawpc.com/6-remedies-breach-of-contract/

2. **Injunctive relief:** In this case, the court will ask someone to stop doing something that they did, which resulted in the breach of a contract. For example, if two parties agreed that certain details shared between them shall remain confidential and yet, one of the parties started sharing such information, the court will ask such a party to stop sharing the information.

3. **Rescission:** This means that the court will let the complaining party cancel the contract so that they would also not keep up with their obligations against the party which committed the breach of contract. For example, if a seller has not delivered the products in accordance with the specifications, the court will allow the buyer to rescind the contract i.e. the buyer need not pay for the goods that were delivered.

4. **Damages:** There are different types of damages that the courts can order to be made payable to the complaining party, in the event that there is a loss caused to such party on account of the breach of the other party.

Quiz

1. Monisha asked Ralph if he would paint her house fence for $200. Ralph replied that if Monisha paid him $350, he would do it. What is missing here in order to create a valid contract?

   a. Offer

   b. Acceptance

   c. Consideration

   d. Legality

2. 12-year-old Jake agreed to mow his neighbor's lawn for $25. Is this a valid contract?

   a. Yes, it is a valid contract.

   b. No, it is not valid because Jake is not of legal age.

   c. No, it is not valid because there are no products sold.

   d. No, it is not valid because the price is too low.

3. Which of the following types of contracts does the UCC provide for?

   a. Sale of a house on the beach

   b. Providing designing services to a business

   c. Sale of 20 boxes of biscuits

   d. Sale of the rights in a book

4. According to the provisions of the UCC, the title of the goods cannot pass to the buyer prior to the:

   a. making of the payment

   b. identification of the goods to the contract

   c. delivery of the goods

   d. packaging of the goods for delivery

5. Which of the following laws provides for the validity of interstate or foreign contracts entered into electronically?

   a. Electronic Funds Transfer Act

   b. ESIGN Act

   c. Regulation Z

   d. ACH Act

6. The condition that a product should be fit for its intended purpose is known as:

   a. saleability

   b. good faith

   c. merchantability

   d. viability

7. **Which of the following is an essential condition for an electronic contract to be entered into under the UETA?**

   a. The electronic contract must mandatorily be followed by a paper version

   b. Both parties must provide their consent to the contract on the same date at the same time

   c. Both parties must consent to the contract being entered into electronically

   d. Both the parties must be located in the same state

8. **A certificate of deposit is a negotiable instrument in the nature of a:**

   a. draft

   b. promissory note

   c. funds transfer

   d. check

9. **Which of the following laws provides for the funds transfers from one bank to another?**

   a. UCC

   b. USC

   c. Regulation ACH

   d. Regulation E

10. When a court stops a party from doing something by virtue of a judgment, it is known as:

   a. specific performance

   b. rescission

   c. damages

   d. injunction

Answers	1 – b	2 – b	3 – c	4 – b	5 – b
	6 – c	7 – c	8 – b	9 – a	10 – d

Chapter Summary

◆ Contracts are required to be entered into in order to bring the terms and conditions of different transactions into writing.

◆ There are some essential elements of a valid contract without the existence of which, the contract may not be enforceable.

◆ The UCC provides for contracts that relate to goods that are tangible and movable while common law also provides for contracts in relation to services, transfer of intellectual property, and real estate.

◆ While electronic contracts are considered to be as legally valid and enforceable as paper contracts, it is essential that the appropriate disclosures have been made and appropriate consents have been obtained. Both parties must agree to enter into a contract electronically.

◆ Payments for contracts can be made either through negotiable instruments or through electronic funds transfers, credit, or debit cards. It is important to know about the modes of payment since depending upon the mode of payment provided for in the contract, it can be known whether the payment was made on time or not.

◆ Contracts can be enforced by invoking the court system i.e. by initiating a legal proceeding. Courts might provide reliefs of specific performance, injunction, rescission, or damages.

This page is intentionally left blank

Chapter **7**

Intellectual Property Law and Intellectual Property Registrations

It takes years for a business to develop a brand. A company has to spend significant time, effort, and money in ensuring that the customers recognize the name and brand of the company. Therefore, it is very important to protect the brand name. The onslaught of the pandemic resulted in increasing use of digital technology and consequently, in the increase of businesses working in the technology domain. These businesses do not have any physical assets. The most valuable asset for them is their intellectual property. If their intellectual property is copied or stolen by someone else, they can lose their most important asset and their business would be significantly impacted. This is why intellectual property needs to be registered, to ensure proprietary or sole ownership and to get the ability to sue someone who copies such intellectual property.

Prior to moving on to understand US laws relating to intellectual property, let's understand what is different about intellectual property laws as compared to laws relating to other matters.

Intellectual property laws are more similar in multiple countries of the world, compared to other matters, because of the World Trade Organization's Trade-Related Aspects of Intellectual Property Rights (TRIPs) Agreement. Prior to this agreement, the protection provided to intellectual property owners was very different in different parts of the world and this caused a lot of issues even in trade between the governments of countries, let alone trade between private businesses.

In order to achieve some common rules relating to intellectual property, the TRIPs agreement was signed by all the members of the World Trade Organization i.e. 164 countries, including the US in 1995. The TRIPs agreement provides for two things: treating foreign nationals in a similar manner as the nationals of that specific country in matters related to intellectual property protection and ensuring that certain minimum standards of protection exist in all countries.

Since the US is also a signatory to the TRIPs agreement, the principles of the protections afforded to different types of intellectual property are similar to other signatory countries.

Key learning objectives of this chapter include the reader's understanding of the following:

- What are the different types of intellectual properties which are recognized by US laws?

- What are trademarks according to US law and what are the benefits of registering them?

- What are the things you can get a patent for in the US and what are the rights associated with a patent?

- What is a copyright according to US laws?

- What does the Digital Millennium Copyright Act provide for?

- What is the role of the US Patents and Trademarks Office in ensuring intellectual property protection?

- How are intellectual properties registered in the US?

Let's dive right in.

7.1 Intellectual Properties Recognized by US Laws

Four main types of intellectual properties are recognized by US laws:

1. Trademarks

2. Patents

3. Copyrights

4. Trade Secrets

There are also specific types of intellectual properties that are covered within the above four main types of intellectual properties, such as design and utility patents, trade dress, geographical indications, and plant variety protection. We will understand what these are, as we discuss each main type below.

7.1.1 Trademarks

When you see this logo, what do you instantly think of?

Everyone instantly recognizes this logo belonging to Apple Inc. This is because, over the years, the company has developed its brand to such an extent that its name and logo are recognized across the world. This is known as a trademark. A trademark can therefore be a name, a logo, a design, or anything which distinguishes the goods sold by a business from other similar products. For example, many companies such as Dell, IBM, etc. sell computers, just like Apple. Unless there was something to distinguish one company's computers from another, it would be very difficult to identify whether a computer was made by Apple or Dell. The branding or the logo on the product makes it possible to identify this. Similarly for services, the name or the logo is known as a "service mark".

In the US, the registration of trademarks is regulated by the Lanham Act (also known as the Trademarks Act).

7.1.2 Patents

Unlike a trademark, a patent is not something related to the product or service itself, like a name or a logo. Instead, a patent is actually a *right* granted by the US Patents and Trademarks Office. Patents are usually granted to inventors or creators, depending on whether it is a utility or a design patent. When someone develops a product that has a unique use, and has not been invented before by anyone else, they can secure a patent for such a product. For example, someone invented a wireless mobile charger when the only chargers available were the ones with a wire. In such a case, they can patent this product since they were the first to think about it and invent it. After such a patent is granted, anyone who manufactures a charger with the same technology must now secure a license from the original inventor to manufacture it.

In the US, Patents are recognized under Title 35 of the United States Code (USC).

7.1.3 Copyrights

A copyright is exactly what the name suggests - a right over any other copies of the creation. It means no one can make any copies of the creation without securing the approval of the creator. Copyrights are used significantly in creational content such as books, movies, or any kind of literary or visual creations, although, interestingly, music can also be secured by copyright. However, it should be noted that copyright only protects the expression of an idea and not the idea itself. This means that if someone made a movie on Abraham Lincoln, it does not prevent other people also from making a movie on Abraham Lincoln, as long as the expressions are different. If you look at an article written by someone, you can still write about the same idea as them, as long as you use completely different words and language to express it. Unlike other intellectual properties, a copyright comes into existence the moment something is created. It is not necessary for any office to grant copyright or for the creator to register the copyright in order for it to be recognized. If you write an article, you have a copyright in it from the moment it is written. Although other people can write on the same idea, they cannot copy or plagiarize the exact article which you have written.

In the US, copyrights are recognized by Title 17 of the United States Code, which includes the Copyright Act of 1976.

7.1.4 Trade Secrets

A trade secret is information that has an actual or potential independent economic value by virtue of not being generally known, has value to others who cannot legitimately obtain this information, and is subject to reasonable efforts to maintain its secrecy.

Let's understand this with the help of an example. Let's assume that there are two companies engaged in the business of manufacturing snacks. During certain seasons, both companies have excessive demand and it is difficult for them to cater to this demand using their current manufacturing resources. Now while experimenting, one of the companies finds a method to speed up the manufacturing process in such a way that it now takes 20% less time to manufacture the same quantity of products as it did before. This can help the company to increase its production and cater to the higher demand. However, its competitor still does not know this method and therefore continues to struggle to manufacture adequate quantities.

This method to speed up the manufacturing can be called a trade secret. It has economic value because the company may be able to get money by guiding other companies to expedite their manufacturing cycle. The company will also ensure that this method is not leaked to other businesses because then, it will lose its competitive advantage.

Similar to copyrights, trade secrets do not need to be registered to be legally protected. Therefore, a company must make adequate internal arrangements to ensure that these are not leaked. This can be done by limiting the secret to only specific employees who need to know it and restricting employees from disclosing it by virtue of their employment agreements.

The Uniform Trade Secrets Act is the law governing trade secrets in the US.

Let's now look at how these intellectual properties can be protected.

7.2 What Can Be Registered as a Trademark and What Are the Benefits of Registering Trademarks?[70]

Any word, phrase, symbol, or design which you use, in order to distinguish your product from other similar products is a trademark. Registering a trademark can give you protection against counterfeiting i.e. someone trying to pass off products manufactured by them as products manufactured by you, and someone trying to copy your logo or brand name.

---

70. *What is a trademark?* Website of the United States Patent and Trademark Office, https://www.uspto.gov/trademarks/basics/what-trademark

When you register a trademark, you have a right to ensure that no one else uses the same or similar trademark in relation to the same or related products or services. It is essential to identify exactly which goods or services your trademark relates to since the more specific you are about the goods or services for which you wish to register the trademark, the higher the chances of it getting registered.

Registering a trademark has certain benefits, which can be listed as under:

1. Registering a trademark places it on a public record. It then becomes a notice to the public that a particular trademark has been registered and that such trademark is, therefore, not available to be used by anyone else in relation to those specific goods or services.

2. When a trademark is registered, it is much easier for you to prove that you own it. Any examination of whether or not you are entitled to register the trademark happens prior to the registration and therefore, once the trademark is registered, it means that you have proved beyond a reasonable doubt to the registering authority that you are entitled to the trademark.

3. You can use the symbol ® against your trademark to make it obvious that the trademark is registered and that it is not available for use to other people in relation to the same or similar goods or services.

4. You can bring a lawsuit against a person who uses the same or similar trademark for the same or similar products or services.

7.3 What Are the Things You Can Get a Patent for in the US and What Are the Rights Associated With a Patent?[71]

A patent can only be obtained for those inventions which are novel, non-obvious, and clearly described and claimed by the inventor. Also, a patent can only be obtained for a process, a machine, an article of manufacture, a composition of matter, or an improvement of any of those.

If an invention has been claimed beforehand or has been published to the world, it cannot be patented. It should also be something non-obvious. This means that someone should not be able to think of it obviously i.e as an obvious improvement or change. Even if it is a new and non-obvious invention, if it has been published somewhere, an inventor will not be able to patent it.

In order to be patented, the invention must be something concrete and not an abstract idea. This means that you must be able to describe or indicate the invention or creation clearly, with all specifications and from all dimensions.

Patents can be of the following types:

1. **Design Patents:** These patents are granted for new, original, and ornamental designs. These patents relate more to the appearance and visual characteristics of an invention rather than the purpose for which it is used. An example of this can be a specific jewelry design.

---

71. *General information concerning Patents,* Website of the United States Patent and Trademark Office, https://www.uspto.gov/patents/basics/general-information-patents

2. **Utility Patents:** These patents are granted for inventions that serve a specific usefulness or purpose. These inventions must be either tangible such as a machine or an article of manufacture or a specific process.

3. **Plant Patents:** Plant patents are granted for inventing or discovering and reproducing a distinct and new variety of a plant.

When you register a patent, you get the right to stop anyone else from commercially exploiting the invention. If anyone else is looking to use your invention for any purpose and looking to earn from it, they would need to secure a license from you. This right is available for a period of 20 years from the date on which the application is filed.

7.4 What Rights Are Included Within a Copyright According to US Laws?[72]

A copyright gives you the right to control the reproduction, distribution, production, or display of your creation. If anyone else wishes to use your creation for any purpose, they need to secure a license from you in order to do that.

Copyrights are available for creations that are artistic, literary, or intellectually created works that are tangible such as novels, movies, music, software, etc.

---

72. *What is Copyright?*, Website of the U.S. Copyright Office, https://www.copyright.gov/what-is-copyright/

7.5 What Does the Digital Millennium Copyright Act Provide For?[73]

The Digital Millennium Copyright Act (DMCA) was passed in order to ensure the protection of creations that are released online. It enables creators to request intermediaries to take the infringing works down, encourages creators to release or publish their creations on the internet, and makes it illegal to provide false copyright management information such as names or authors, copyright owners, or titles of work or to remove or alter that information.

The takedown mechanism is the most important element of the DMCA. Under this mechanism, all intermediary websites are mandated to provide information to the users as to where they can reach, in order to request something to be taken down from the website in the event of a copyright infringement.

Hence, if a creator finds that his or her creation is being copied by someone else online, they can send a takedown notice to the relevant intermediary who would have to take down the infringing work.

For example, if you find that someone copied your video and placed it on YouTube, you can submit a copyright removal request to YouTube here - https://support.google.com/youtube/answer/2807622?hl=en

This is helpful because it gives creators assurance that their online creations are protected to a certain extent. In the absence of such a mechanism, people will easily copy and gain from other people's works.

---

73. *The Digital Millennium Copyright Act,* Website of the U.S. Copyright Office, https://www.copyright.gov/dmca/

7.6 What is the Role of the United States Patents and Trademarks Office in Ensuring Intellectual Property Protection?[74]

The United States Patents and Trademarks Office (USPTO) is the federal agency that is responsible for granting patents and registering trademarks. Once a patent is granted by the USPTO and a trademark is registered with it, the inventors or brand owners have their intellectual property protected throughout the US.

The interesting thing is that the filing of patent applications and filing applications for registration of trademarks can be completed by the inventors or brand owners themselves, and for this purpose, the USPTO provides elaborate guidance through various guides or videos to enable the inventors or brand owners to file their applications.

Furthermore, the details of the patents granted and trademarks registered as well as the applications filed are publicly available on the website of the USPTO and the USPTO also provides guidance on how to search for the details of these. This is extremely helpful to potential inventors and business owners who wish to know whether a brand name has already been registered.

In addition to the above, the USPTO also advises the President of the US, the Secretary of Commerce, and the US Government on intellectual property protection and enforcement.

---

74. *About Us,* Website of the U.S. Patents and Trademark Office, https://www.uspto.gov/about-us

7.7 Registration of Intellectual Properties

Let's say you are based in Houston, Texas and have invented a new kind of remote control. Together with this device, you also want to register the name of the brand - Self Starter remotes. What do you need to do to register it?

In the US, it is possible for you to register your trademark or apply for a patent at both state and federal levels. However, when you file for a patent or apply to register a trademark at a state level, the protection that you receive is limited to the specific state. On the other hand, if you file for a patent or apply to register a trademark with the USPTO, the protection extends to the entire US.

Filing an application for registration of a trademark with the USPTO is expensive compared to registration of a trademark with the state registration offices. For instance, if you were to apply for the registration of a trademark with the Texas Secretary of State, the cost would be $50 per class, while with the USPTO, the minimum cost would be $250 per class. However, in view of the fact that the registration offers protection at a national level, most brand name owners choose to file the application with the USPTO.

7.7.1 Process for registering trademarks

Here's what the basic process for registering a trademark with the USPTO looks like:

Applications for registering a trademark are made online. In order to complete the application, one of the most important things you will need is to know the classification under which your product or service falls. Fortunately, the USPTO provides elaborate guidance on the classification codes which are required to be used for the application.

 This guidance can be found here - https://www. uspto.gov/trademarks/search/get-ready-search-classification-and-design

It might take as much as six months for the application to progress to the examination stage. It is important to keep monitoring the status of the application on the Trademark Status and Document Retrieval System.

At the stage of examination, the examining attorney will check if the application complies with the applicable laws and if the examining attorney believes that the application should be refused, the examining attorney will send a response to that effect explaining the reasons why the application should not be accepted. If the examining attorney believes minor corrections to be necessary, even in that case, the examining attorney shall send an office action.

The office action needs to be responded to and thereafter, the trademark is approved for publication in the official gazette. Once it is published in the official gazette, if anyone wants to oppose the registration of the mark, they have 30 days to file an opposition. Within a period of three to four months from the date of publication, if the trademark application has been filed on the basis of use, the mark will be registered and a certificate of registration will be issued.

7.7.2 Process for registering patents[75]

The first thing that would need to be done is to determine whether or not the product is patentable, as we discussed earlier in the chapter. If the product is indeed patentable, an application needs to be filed for the grant of a patent. Patent applications require a bit of effort and are not as simple as trademark applications. This is because patent applications require the description of the product in significant detail. Once the application is filed, if it is complete, the application will move to the examination stage, and if the examiner believes that the application meets the requirements, the applicant will receive a Notice of Approval.

---

75. *Patent Process Overview*, Website of the United States Patent and Trademark Office, https://www.uspto.gov/patents/basics/patent-process-overview#step6

Quiz

━━━

1. **Software codes can be registered as:**

   a. patents

   b. trademarks

   c. copyrights

   d. trade secrets

2. **Which of the following is not required to be registered in order to be legally protected?**

   a. Design Patents

   b. Utility Patents

   c. Service Marks

   d. Trade Secrets

3. **If a company finds a better way to market its products, thus giving it a competitive advantage, this will be considered a:**

   a. service mark

   b. design patent

   c. copyright

   d. trade secret

4. **One of the most important provisions of the Digital Millennium Copyright Act is the:**

   a. removal mechanism

   b. infringement mechanism

   c. takedown mechanism

   d. passing off mechanism

5. **Which of the following can you obtain a patent for in the US?**

   a. A book

   b. A new design for television which is not an obvious improvement

   c. An idea about how the world can be a better place

   d. A song

6. **In order to make an application for a trademark, you must know the:**

   a. designing cost of the trademark

   b. number of users of your product or service

   c. classification under which your product or service falls

   d. MRP of your product or service

7. **You can check the status of your trademark application on the:**

   a. trademark watch system

   b. trademarks application and approval system

   c. trademarks search and approval system

   d. trademark status and document retrieval system

8. **An "office action" is:**

   a. a response from the USPTO on the trademark application

   b. an action taken by the USPTO to cancel a trademark registration

   c. an approval of registration of a trademark

   d. an action taken by the USPTO against infringement of a trademark

9. **The law governing the use of trade secrets is:**

   a. The Trade Secrets Code

   b. The Uniform Trade Secrets Act

   c. Title 18 of the United States Code

   d. Title 4 of the Uniform Commercial Code

10. After an application has been filed for claiming a Patent, the next stage in the process is:

   a. approval

   b. description

   c. publication

   d. examination

Answers	1 – c	2 – d	3 – d	4 – c	5 – b
	6 – c	7 – d	8 – a	9 – a	10 – d

Chapter Summary

◆ Intellectual property laws are different as compared to laws relating to other matters because countries that were a signatory to the TRIPs agreement agreed to have certain standard protections in place for intellectual properties and hence the laws end up being similar.

◆ Under US laws, the types of intellectual properties recognized are trademarks, patents, copyrights, and trade secrets.

◆ A trademark registration acts as a public notice of the ownership of the trademark and gives the owner the right to ensure that no one else uses the same or similar trademark for the same or similar products.

◆ A patent is granted for new and non-obvious inventions which are concrete and not for abstract ideas or thoughts.

◆ Unlike the other types of intellectual property, copyright and trade secrets do not require to be registered in order to be legally valid.

◆ The USPTO is the federal agency responsible for the registration of trademarks and granting patents.

◆ Intellectual properties can be registered at the state level as well as at the federal level, however, at the state level, the protection is afforded only within the state, while an application with the USPTO affords national-level protection to the intellectual property.

◆ The registration process for both trademarks and patents involves the main stages of application, examination, and registration or approval.

This page is intentionally left blank

Chapter 8

Data Protection and Privacy Laws

The relevance of data protection and privacy increased manifold during the pandemic years. This is because the requirement to stay at home brought the maximum number of people on the internet. But the devices used by people in their homes do not usually have the kind of security mechanisms that companies have. Not only that, online businesses increased in number and size. Many of these businesses collect data from their customers and it is often sensitive data.

[76]Prior to understanding the laws relating to data protection in the US, let us first understand some main principles of data protection laws:

---

76. *Principles of Data Protection,* Website of the Data Protection Commission in Ireland, https://www.dataprotection.ie/en/individuals/data-protection-basics/principles-data-protection

1. **Lawfulness, fairness, and transparency:** This principle provides that you can collect data from someone only

   a. with their consent, or

   b. pursuant to a contract with them, or

   c. to meet an obligation which the law has cast on you or

   d. if it is vital for the protection of interest of the person whose data you are collecting, or

   e. it is essential to protect the public interest or another legitimate interest.

   Fairness and transparency mean that the person collecting the data must make it clear and open to the person whose data is being collected as to what their data will be used for.

2. **Purpose limitation:** Not only should you make it explicit to the people whose data you are collecting what purpose you will use the data for, but also there should be no deviation in the actual use from the stated purpose. The data should be used for the exact purpose for which it is stated it will be used.

3. **Data minimization:** Only the data which is necessary for a required purpose should be collected and not any additional data.

4. **Accuracy:** The data that is collected should be accurate. Inaccurate data should be erased. The data system should ensure that there is a periodical deletion of data so that outdated data is not stored in the system.

5. **Storage limitation:** According to this principle, the data should only be stored for as long as necessary and should not be stored for a longer period of time.

6. **Integrity and confidentiality:** The person who collects the data is required to maintain its confidentiality and ensure that it's not leaked.

7. **Accountability:** It means that you need to be responsible for every step of the data processing that happens with the data that you collect.

These basic principles govern the data protection laws in most countries including the US.

In the US, in addition to general data protection and privacy laws prevalent in the different states, there are federal laws relating to privacy in sectors where it is possible that a large amount of personal data will be secured, such as healthcare service providers or schools. We will discuss both the federal laws relating to different sectors and the state laws.

Key learning objectives of this chapter include the reader's understanding of the following:

- What are the different types of federal laws related to data protection relating to the privacy of:

    - Health information

    - Consumer reporting

    - Student records

    - Websites and online services directed at children

- Customers of financial institutions

- Electronic communications

- People who purchase or rent audio-visual material

- What are the main features of state privacy laws in the states of:

  - California

  - New York

  - Colorado

  - Pennsylvania

  - Ohio and

  - Virginia

Let's now discuss all of these laws in a little more detail.

8.1 Health Insurance Portability and Accountability Act of 1996 (HIPAA)[77]

The information about a person's health is quite sensitive and personal. Such personal information gets frequently relayed to healthcare service providers. The HIPAA is aimed at protecting the privacy of such sensitive information about the patients

---

77. *Health Insurance Portability and Accountability Act,* Office of the Assistant Secretary for Planning and Evaluation, U.S. Department of Health and Human Services, https://aspe.hhs.gov/reports/health-insurance-portability-accountability-act-1996

and preventing any dealing with such information without the patient's consent or knowledge.

8.1.1 Applicability

The HIPAA applies to "covered entities". These covered entities include healthcare service providers, health insurers and health maintenance organizations, healthcare clearinghouses, and business associates.

Furthermore, the HIPAA provides standards to deal with medical records and other individually identifiable health information, together defined as "protected health information" or PHI under the HIPAA.

8.1.2 Key provisions

There are five relevant rules that the HIPAA requires the covered entities to follow:

1. **Privacy rule:** This rule requires the covered entities to:

   a. put in place appropriate safeguards to protect PHI

   b. ensure that the PHI is not used or disclosed beyond permitted limits unless this is done with the permission of the relevant individual

   This rule also gives individuals certain rights to their PHI. They can examine, copy, request corrections, and ask for PHI to be forwarded to such persons as they may inform.

2. **Security rule:** This rule lays down certain national standards which are required to be implemented by the covered entities in terms of specific administrative, physical,

and technical safeguards to ensure that the PHI received, used, or maintained by covered entities is protected.

3. **Enforcement rule:** This rule provides for compliance and investigations, imposition of penalties for violation, and procedures for hearings.

4. **Breach notification rule**: This rule requires covered entities to provide a notification for the breach i.e. a leak of unsecured PHI.

5. **Omnibus rule:** This rule brought in many provisions of the Health Information Technology for Economic and Clinical Health (HITECH) Act within the HIPAA to ensure the security and protection of PHI.

8.1.3 Penalties[78]

The penalties under the HIPAA are divided on the basis of the severity of the offense. The division is as follows:

Table 8.1

Type of violation	Penalty
An unknown violation which could have been avoided with reasonable care	Minimum fine of $100 per violation, up to $50,000
Violation which could have been known, but could not have been avoided with reasonable care	Minimum fine of $1000 per violation, up to $50,000

---

78. *What are the Penalties for HIPAA Violations?,* Website of the HIPAA Journal, https://www.hipaajournal.com/what-are-the-penalties-for-hipaa-violations-7096/

Type of violation	Penalty
Violation which was caused due to "wilful neglect", but an attempt was made to correct it	Minimum fine of $10,000 per violation, up to $50,000
Violation which was caused due to "wilful neglect" and no attempt was made to correct it	Minimum fine of $50,000 per violation

These penalties are derived from the HITECH Act and are adjusted for inflation.

8.2 Fair Credit Reporting Act[79]

A lot of information about people can be available with consumer reporting companies which collect information in order to furnish it to:

- lenders who want to know about the creditworthiness of borrowers

- companies that want to hire employees and need to know their background

- landlords who want to rent property and want to know the credibility of a tenant

- insurance companies who want to determine the risks in insuring people

---

79. *Fair Credit Reporting Act,* Website of the U.S. Federal Trade Commission, https://www.ftc.gov/legal-library/browse/statutes/fair-credit-reporting-act

and other such companies who need bulk information for business purposes. This is why certain standards need to be prescribed for dealing with information by such companies.

8.2.1 Applicability

This act applies to consumer reporting companies such as credit bureaus, medical reporting companies, and tenant screening agencies. It also provides for a very wide definition of "consumer reports" which include all kinds of information collected by consumer reporting agencies that is to be used for the purpose of decision-making by companies to grant credit, insurance, employment, etc.

8.2.2 Key provisions

1. Consumer reporting agencies are only permitted to provide a consumer report in accordance with the law, in accordance with instructions of the consumer, or in accordance with the request from a third party for a legitimate business purpose. Even where such reports are provided, there are prescribed conditions that need to be followed for the provision of the reports.

2. The consumer reports cannot include certain prescribed information such as bankruptcy, civil or criminal proceedings, tax liens, or accounting-related details which are older than 7 years. Medical information also cannot be included except where certain details are restricted or the report is being provided to an insurance company.

3. There are provisions to curtail identity theft by requiring consumer reporting companies to install fraud alerts and blocking information.

4. This act also provides for compliance procedures to be put in place and disclosures required to be made by consumer reporting companies.

8.2.3 Penalties

The following is the penalty structure under this act:

Table 8.2

Type of violation	Penalty
Wilful failure to comply with any requirement relating to a consumer and if obtaining a consumer report under false pretense	Minimum $100, maximum $1000
	$1000 or damage sustained by consumer whichever is greater Plus: Punitive damages allowed by the court; and costs of action including attorney's costs

8.3 Family Educational Rights and Privacy Act (FERPA)[80]

Schools have access to a significant amount of data relating to the children enrolled in the schools. This is necessary in order to confirm the identity of the child and to ensure medical attention in case of any emergencies during school hours. However, the way in which this data is handled becomes even more crucial since it relates to minors.

8.3.1 Applicability

Interestingly, the FERPA applies to all schools and educational institutions which secure funds from a program approved by the Department of Education in the US and which are actually providing educational services. This would probably leave private schools which do not receive any funding out of the scope, however, in such cases, the private schools might become subject to the state-specific data protection laws.

8.3.2 Key provisions

This act gives certain specific rights to the parents of students who are minors and to adult students themselves in relation to their information which is stored with the school. Parents of minor students or adult students can:

- Inspect and review the student records

---

80. *34 CFR Part 99, Family Educational Rights and Privacy,* Website of the U.S. Department of Education, https://studentprivacy.ed.gov/node/548/#0.1_se34.1.99_160d

- Request correction to the records if they believe the records to be inaccurate or misleading

The schools can only share the information relating to the students with the permission of the parents (in case of a minor student) or the student if they are adults. However, they are permitted to share information in certain cases such as for the purpose of transfer to other schools, to appropriate officials in the case of an emergency, to comply with a judicial order, to state authorities within a juvenile justice system according to state law, etc. But even these express permissions are subject to conditions.

8.3.3 Penalties

The highest penalty for non-compliance with FERPA is that the Secretary of the Department of Education can terminate the funding that is made available to the school or educational institution under the Department of Education program.

8.4 Children's Online Privacy Protection Act (COPPA)[81]

Even very young children have access to the internet nowadays, if not for entertainment, then for online education. K-12 or kindergarten to 12th-grade education is a huge market for online education businesses. In addition to this, there can be many websites such as learning arts and crafts or gaming, or even social media platforms that children can be accessing and can be

---

81. *15 U.S.C. 6901, Chapter 91: Children's Online Privacy Protection,* http://uscode.house. gov/view.xhtml?req=granuleid%3AUSC-prelim-title15-section6501&edition=prelim

providing their information. It is essential that such websites are regulated in order to ensure the protection and privacy of such information.

8.4.1 Applicability

The COPPA applies to operators of commercial websites or other online services directed to children under 13 years of age. Those websites or online services where only a specific part of the website or online services are directed at children are also covered.

8.4.2 Key provisions

Unlike other statutes which regulate dealing with information, COPPA places restrictions on collecting the information itself. The operators of websites or online services directed at children are required to obtain what is known as "verifiable parental consent" prior to collecting, using, or disclosing the personal information of the children.

8.4.3 Penalties

The penalties for violations in COPPA are the same as for violations of any rules related to unfair trade practices. These are laid down in Sections 5(l) and 5(m) of the Federal Trade Commission (FTC) Act. These penalties are inflation adjusted, and for 2022, the penalty for violation can be up to $46,517 per violation.[82] If a website is not careful, it can end up paying extensive penalties.

---

82. *Inflation-Adjusted Civil Penalty Amounts,* Federal Trade Commission, https://www.ftc.gov/news-events/news/press-releases/2022/01/ftc-publishes-inflation-adjusted-civil-penalty-amounts-2022

In 2019, Google and YouTube had to pay a massive amount of $170 million to the FTC as a settlement amount for violations of COPPA.[83] This was mainly because Youtube used tracking cookies (identifiers that can track the internet behaviour of a user, in this case, children) to direct targeted ads to users. However, this was not disclosed and parental consent was not obtained for this tracking.

8.5 Gramm-Leach-Bliley Act or Financial Services Modernization Act[84]

Banks and finance companies such as companies offering loans, investment advisory services or brokers, insurance companies, etc. (commonly known as BFSI - banking, financial services, and insurance) are other types of entities which are a repository to a large amount of information about the customers and a lot of this information can be sensitive such as data relating to the income, investment appetite, etc. of people.

However, unlike the previous laws that we discussed, the Gramm-Leach-Bliley Act (GLBA) is not actually a data privacy legislation. It was enacted to facilitate mergers and acquisitions in the BFSI sector and enable "financial holding companies" to carry out what it calls "activities which are financial in nature". It is also not a part of the United States Code.

---

83. *Google and YouTube Will Pay Record $170 Million for Alleged Violations of Children's Privacy Law,* Press Releases of the Federal Trade Commission, https://www.ftc.gov/news-events/news/press-releases/2019/09/google-youtube-will-pay-record-170-million-alleged-violations-childrens-privacy-law

84. *Gramm-Leach-Bliley Act,* U.S. Government Information Website, https://www.govinfo.gov/content/pkg/PLAW-106publ102/pdf/PLAW-106publ102.pdf

However, as we noted above, considering the massive amount of data that these companies hold, Title V of the GLBA contains strict provisions relating to the protection of non-public personal information.

8.5.1 Applicability

The privacy-related provisions of GLBA apply to all financial institutions. The term "financial institution" has been very widely defined as any financial institution which is engaged in the business of providing financial services to customers who maintain a credit, deposit, trust, or other financial account or relationship with the institution.

8.5.2 Key provisions

1. **The Financial Privacy Rule:** This rule requires that financial institutions comply with certain limitations on the disclosure of non-public personal information. The financial institutions must also provide a notice to the customer of their privacy policies and how the information is shared with their affiliates or other third parties and what they do with it. They must also give the customer a chance to opt-out so that their information is not disclosed to anyone else.

2. **The Safeguards Rule:** Financial institutions are required to develop, install, and maintain an information security program that has proper administrative, technical, and physical safeguards to protect non-public personal information. This is required because given the volume of personal information that these entities handle, privacy protection has to be built within the system and cannot be

something that is deployed on an ad-hoc basis. Not only that they have to maintain the program, but also it must be appropriate to the size and complexity of the business.

3. **Pretexting:** Financial institutions are also required to ensure that the personal information that they possess is protected against disclosure on account of false pretenses such as scams, social engineering, etc.

8.5.3 Penalties

Breach of GLBA has severe penalties. It can result in imprisonment of 5 years for anyone who knowingly violates or attempts to violate the provisions of the GLBA. For offenses where there is a pattern of violation - other laws being violated together with GLBA, the penalty can be imprisonment for up to 10 years. Even the amounts of fines are high since the maximum fine prescribed for a felony is $250,000, and that for misdemeanor not resulting in death is $100,000.

8.6 Electronic Communications Privacy Act (ECPA)[85]

This legislation is not focused on managing data received, but rather on obtaining data in an illegal manner. This act is also known as the Wiretap Act and it prohibits any kind of interception of wire, oral, or electronic communication.

---

85. *Electronic Communications Privacy Act of 1986*, Bureau of Justice Assistance, U.S. Department of Justice, https://bja.ojp.gov/program/it/privacy-civil-liberties/authorities/statutes/1285

8.6.1 Applicability

This act does not restrict itself in application to a specific category of people or institutions but rather applies to specific actions.

8.6.2 Key provisions

This act prohibits the intentional actual or attempted interception of any oral, wire, or electronic communication by anyone. It also prohibits producing any communication procured illegally from being presented as evidence.

However, one of the laid down exceptions to this is where an employer intercepts communications by employees in the normal course of employment. For example, time tracking devices which track how much time has been spent on a specific activity by an employee might be normal if the employee is being paid on an hourly basis or the intention is to increase the efficiency of work. The other exception is where persons authorized by law intercept such communications in order to conduct surveillance.

8.6.3 Penalties

Anyone who illegally intercepts communication can be liable to pay damages to the person whose communication was intercepted. Not only this but also the court can impose punitive damages and may also subject the offender to imprisonment for a period of 5 years.

8.7 Video Privacy Protection Act (VPPA)[86]

The intention of the VPPA was basically to prohibit sharing of information to allow targeted advertising. When advertisers know your preferences i.e. the things you like, this is very crucial information for them, since they will surround you with advertisements accordingly so that you end up buying. Whoever collects this kind of information, in this case, the video service providers, therefore, can sell it to the advertisers for a lot of money.

8.7.1 Applicability

The VPPA applies to video service providers. However, this act was enacted in 1988, when people approached video service providers to rent video cassettes or DVDs. For now, this kind of service is provided by digital streaming services which allow you to rent movies directly on the internet. Since the act extends to the provision of "similar other audiovisual materials" in addition to "video cassette tapes", even the streaming service providers are covered.

These service providers cannot provide personal data about who purchased which movies or other audio-visual materials to anyone without consent. However, in order to apply, the information must be personally identifiable i.e. it should state that X person purchased Y movie. If it provides general information i.e. someone in Nevada purchased a thriller action movie, this would not be covered, since it is generalized information.

---

86. *Video Privacy Protection Act of 1988,* Website of the United States Congress, https://www.congress.gov/bill/100th-congress/senate-bill/2361

8.7.2 Key provisions

1. As discussed before, video service providers are prohibited
    from sharing specific information about the rental of video
    cassettes and other audio-visual materials under this act.

2. They are permitted to share such information only with the
    consumers themselves or with their consent or if so required
    by a warrant, subpoena, or court order.

3. An interesting fact is that disclosure is permitted if such
    disclosure is incident to the ordinary course of business of
    the video tape service provider.

8.7.3 Penalties

While there are no specific penalties, the act allows a person
who is aggrieved by a violation of this act to bring an action for
damages and the court may allow damages together with attorney
costs.

8.8 State Laws Relating to Data Protection and Privacy

As of August 2022, only five states in the US had signed laws
relating to privacy - California, Colorado, Virginia, Connecticut,
and Utah.[87] Some other states such as Michigan, Pennsylvania,
New Jersey, and Ohio had active bills on privacy laws.

---

87. *U.S. State Privacy Legislation Tracker,* Website of the International Association of
Privacy Professionals, https://iapp.org/media/pdf/resource_center/State_Comp_
Privacy_Law_Chart.pdf

8.8.1 California

California was the first state to enact a detailed privacy legislation in the form of the California Consumer Privacy Act (CCPA), which grants consumers significant control over their data.

The CCPA is a landmark legislation, not only because it is the first enacted privacy legislation in a US state, but also because it can be seen as a business-friendly version of GDPR.[88]

Following are some interesting features of the CCPA:

1. The CCPA applies only to businesses that are for-profit and have an annual revenue of over $25 million, process personal information of at least 50,000 consumers, and derive 50% or more annual revenues from selling personal information. This definition excludes a lot of smaller businesses from the scope.

2. A "consumer" is defined as a natural person who is a California resident. This means that businesses that process data of persons who are not residents of California are not covered.

3. Some of the main rights given to consumers in relation to their personal information are the right to know which of their information is being collected and shared, the right to opt out of the sale of their personal information, and the right to request deletion of their personal information.

4. Covered businesses are required to provide a clear link or button on their website that states "Do Not Sell My Personal

---

88. *California Consumer Privacy Act, of 2018,* Website of the Legislature of California, https://leginfo.legislature.ca.gov/faces/codes_displayText.xhtml?division=3.&part=4.&lawCode=CIV&title=1.81.5

Information", allowing the consumers to opt out of the sale of their personal information. The businesses cannot require a consumer to open an account with them for submitting this request. Users can also act themselves to install controls like Global Privacy Control (GPC) on their devices, which automatically signals to the businesses that the user does not wish to enable selling their personal information.[89]

5. The businesses are also required to give certain notices to the consumers, including their privacy policy.

8.8.2 New York

As of August 2022, the New York Privacy Act is still in the form of a Bill before the New York Senate and hasn't been enacted. [90]

Some of the rights that the Bill provides for are the right to know how their data is being processed and sold, the right to opt out, ability to access and obtain copies of data handled by the business, the ability to request correction of data as well as deletion of data, etc.

This act defines data controllers and data processors and requires data processors to conduct regular assessments of processing activities and controllers to notify the consumers of any interest that may be harmed before requesting their consent to deal with their data.

---

89. Website of Global Privacy Control, https://globalprivacycontrol.org/

90. Senate Bill S6701B, Website of the NY State Senate, https://www.nysenate.gov/legislation/bills/2021/S6701

8.8.3 Colorado

Colorado was the third state after California and Virginia to sign a privacy law into an act.

[91]The Colorado Privacy Act applies to data controllers conducting business in Colorado or who produce or deliver products or services which are targeted to residents of Colorado with the additional conditions that:

- such controllers control or process the personal data of one hundred thousand or more consumers; or

- derives revenue from or receives a discount on the price of goods or services from the sale of personal data and processes or controls personal data of 25,000 or more consumers.

It also provides certain rights to consumers such as the right to opt out of the sale of their information, the right of access to their information, the right to request correction of their information, the right to request deletion of their information, and the right to request their information in portable devices.

8.8.4 Pennsylvania

Pennsylvania is yet to enact privacy legislation, but in April 2021, a bill was introduced in the Pennsylvania General Assembly to enact the Consumer Data Privacy Act (CDPA).[92]

---

91. *Senate Bill 21-190,* Website of the Colorado General Assembly, https://leg.colorado. gov/sites/default/files/2021a_190_signed.pdf

92. *House Bill 1126,* Website of the Pennsylvania General Assembly, https://www.legis. state.pa.us/cfdocs/billInfo/billInfo.cfm?sYear=2021&sInd=0&body=H&type=B&bn=1126

Following suit of the CCPA, the CDPA applies to businesses that have annual gross revenues in excess of $10,000,000 or which buy or receive personal information of 50,000 or more consumers, or which derive 50% or more of annual revenues from selling consumers' personal information.

It gives certain rights to the consumers such as the right to know what personal information is being collected about them, to whom it is being sold or disclosed, the right to opt out of the sale of their information, to access their information, and to expect equal treatment despite them exercising their rights under this act.

8.8.5 Virginia

The Consumer Data Protection Act of Virginia takes on the definitions of covered entities from the HIPAA and imposes responsibilities on the controllers of data to limit the collection of data to what is required, not process personal data unless reasonably required, establish and maintain adequate data security practices, etc.

If a controller sells data for targeted advertising, the controller has to clearly disclose such sales and provide a manner in which a consumer may opt out of such sales.

The consumers have rights to access their data, confirm whether a controller is processing their personal data, correct inaccuracies, request deletion, opt out of the processing, and obtain a copy of the data with the controller.

Quiz

1. **To which of the following does the HIPAA not apply?**

   a. Healthcare service providers

   b. Healthcare insurers

   c. Healthcare publications

   d. Healthcare clearinghouses

2. **The Data minimization principle of the GDPR provides that:**

   a. out of the data collected, minimal data should be sold

   b. only necessary data should be collected

   c. only data of a minimal section of consumers should be collected

   d. only minimal data should be made available to third parties

3. **The Family Educational Rights and Privacy Act is applicable to:**

   a. schools which collect data of parents

   b. schools which receive funds from a program of Department of Education

   c. schools which are established by non-governmental organizations

   d. schools which are specially for children of veterans

4. **COPPA applies to operators of commercial websites or online services directed at children under ___ years of age.**

   a. 13

   b. 15

   c. 16

   d. 18

5. **Pretexting requirements under GLBA require financial institutions to:**

   a. not secure information from consumers under different pretexts

   b. not to sell the information of the consumers under different pretexts

   c. process information only on the correct pretext

   d. protect information from false pretenses such as social engineering

6. **Wire-tapping is prohibited under the:**

   a. Electronic Communications Privacy Act

   b. Gramm-Leach-Bliley Act

   c. Video Privacy Protection Act

   d. Children's Online Privacy Protection Act

7. **If you are an online streaming service company, which of the following legislations will apply to you?**

   a. Electronic Communications Privacy Act

   b. Gramm-Leach-Bliley Act

   c. Video Privacy Protection Act

   d. Children's Online Privacy Protection Act

8. **The CCPA applies to businesses which are for-profit and have an annual revenue of over _____.**

   a. $50,000

   b. $25 million

   c. $100,000

   d. $10 million

9. **_____ was the second state to enact privacy legislation after California.**

   a. New York

   b. Hawaii

   c. Pennsylvania

   d. Virginia

10. **Which of the following legislations would apply to lenders who want to know the creditworthiness of borrowers?**

    a. Gramm-Leach-Bliley Act

    b. Electronic Communications Privacy Act

    c. Fair Credit Reporting Act

    d. Financial Credit Reporting Act

Answers	1 – c	2 – b	3 – b	4 – a	5 – d
	6 – a	7 – c	8 – b	9 – d	10 – c

Chapter Summary

◆ At the federal level, the US privacy and data protection legislations regulate entities that are likely to have access to and process large amounts of personal data such as banks and financial institutions, medical service providers, schools, etc.

◆ However, certain legislations such as the ECPA and VPPA deal more with regulating the obtaining and processing of personal data.

◆ Legislations such as HIPAA and GLBA provide for the establishment of adequate safeguards by the entities processing personal data.

◆ Many legislations have heavy penalties for the breach of provisions relating to privacy and the penalties prescribed are inflation adjusted.

◆ California was the first state in the US to enact a privacy law and the CCPA is considered to be a landmark legislation since it is viewed as a business-friendly version of the GDPR.

◆ Virginia, Colorado, and Connecticut are the only other states which have enacted a privacy law.

This page is intentionally left blank

Chapter **9**

Real Estate Laws

Real estate transactions mainly relate to the purchase and sale of real estate or the leasing, licensing, or renting of real estate. In many countries, secondary market transactions i.e. transactions related to buying and selling residential or commercial property which is already constructed tend to be largely contract driven i.e. based on the terms between two parties. These transactions are therefore not regulated by specific laws relating to real estate, but rather by laws relating to the contracts. For example, if a person wishes to sell their house property at a specific price, the law will not interfere with whether that is the right price for the property or not, because it is up to the seller and the buyer to determine this.

However, there can be laws relating to disclosures about the real estate being transferred (referred to as "conveyance" of property) and the manner in which these contracts are to be executed and recorded, and laws relating to the functioning of real estate brokers and agents who are involved in facilitating these transactions.

These transactions are largely regulated at a state level and not a federal level. This is because the states are very different in terms of area, the density of population, etc. The states tax real estate transactions differently too. At a federal level, the laws relate only to the Public Lands (Title 43 of the United States Code) and Fair Housing (Fair Housing Act).

Key learning objectives of this chapter include the reader's understanding of the following:

- What are federal laws relating to real estate and some interesting provisions of the USC relating to Public Lands and the Fair Housing Act?

- What are the laws relating to purchase and sale of land prevalent in California, Texas, New York, and Hawaii, - states that have a higher number of property transactions?

- How are landlord - tenant relationships regulated in these states?

- What are the laws relating to licensing of real estate brokers and agents as prevalent in these states?

9.1 Federal Laws Relating to Real Estate

Given the geographical and economic diversity in the states, the federal laws do not aim at regulating real estate privately owned by residents in a particular state, since at the federal level, only matters related to the public interest, in general, are regulated. We will therefore discuss two areas of federal law where public interests are involved - relating to public lands and fair housing.

9.1.1 Provisions of Title 43 of the USC relating to Public Lands

"Public lands" have been defined inclusively in Chapter 6 of this title as including federal lands, outer continental shelf, and waters off the coasts of the territories of Alaska and Hawaii.

The provisions of Chapter 6 of Title 43 enable the withdrawal of public lands by the Department of Defense for specific projects. The land would then cease to be public and will be used by the Department of Defense. If such land is more than 5,000 acres, this can only be done by an application to the Congress.

This Title also provides for the United States Geological Survey, changes to land offices in certain districts, and Chapter 35, which deals with ongoing identification of public lands and land use planning.

9.2 Fair Housing Act

The Fair Housing Act (42 USC 3601 onwards) prohibits discrimination on the grounds of race, religion, color, sex, family status, or disability by housing providers such as landlords, real estate companies, and municipalities or entities which provide funds for housing such as banks and financial institutions. However, religious organizations or private clubs are not covered by this prohibition.

The Secretary of Housing and Urban Development is responsible for administering this act. However, the enforcement of this act is only on the basis of a complaint of discrimination. If a complaint is made, this act provides for the procedure to be followed for investigation and conciliation.

9.3 State Laws Relating to Real Estate

9.3.1 California: Real Estate Law, Subdivided Lands Law and Vacation Ownership and Time-Share Act of 2004[93]

The law relating to real estate in California is covered under Division 4 of the Business and Professions Code and contains provisions related to licensing of brokers and real estate salespersons, listing agents and appraisers, their activities and payments to them and provides for establishing a Real Estate Commissioner who is responsible for enforcement of provisions relating to licensees to ensure maximum protection for the buyers.

It provides that no one can act as a real estate broker or real estate salesperson without obtaining a license in this regard. In order to secure this license, it is necessary for people to pass an examination conducted by the Department of Real Estate in California.[94] An application is required to be made to the Real Estate Commissioner even for the purpose of appearing for this

---

93. *Real Estate Law, Subdivided Lands Law And Vacation Ownership and Time-Share Act of 2004,* Website of the California Department of Real Estate, https://dre.ca.gov/files/pdf/relaw/2022/relaw.pdf

94. *Details for DRE Licensing Exams,* Website of the California Department of Real Estate, https://www.dre.ca.gov/Examinees/

examination. In addition to qualifying for this examination, brokers or real estate salespersons are also required to undergo a course at accredited institutions covering real estate practice, legal aspects of real estate, real estate financing, business law, etc. These licenses are valid for a period of four years and can be renewed.

In addition to real estate brokers and salespersons, California law also provides for licensing and certification of appraisers and common interest development managers, who manage specified residential developments.

California is often referred to as the "golden state" for real estate and in accordance with the law relating to real estate, the lands in California which are proposed to be divided for the purpose of sale are referred to as "subdivided" lands. In addition to the lands, under the code, the term "subdivided lands" also includes planned development, community apartment projects, or condominium projects containing five or more units.

As we discussed before, most secondary market sales tend to be contract-driven, but that is why California provides for the qualification and regulation of the intermediaries who support such contracts, rather than regulating the contracts themselves. The only provision in relation to sales contracts is that the sales contracts for real property are required to clearly lay down the description of the property, the terms of the contract, and the encumbrances on the property as of the date of the contract.

For the purposes of the sale or transfer of property in California, a grant deed is required to be drawn up in most circumstances and such deed is required to be notarised.[95] It is also recommended that the deed be recorded with the relevant

95. *Property Ownership and Deed Recording,* Website of the California State Board of Equalization, https://www.boe.ca.gov/proptaxes/pdf/Ownership_DeedRecording.pdf

county clerk/recorder.[96]

California code on real estate law also provides for vacation or "time-share" ownerships, which basically means that multiple people can buy and use a property as a vacation home for a specific time period. This enables people to use luxury homes because the ownership is divided between many people, thus making it affordable for people to use it during vacation time.

9.3.2 California: Tenant Protection Act of 2019[97]

This division of the Business and Professions Code also governs the relationship between landlords and tenants and is proposed to be in force for a period of ten years from January 1, 2020, to January 1, 2030. It provides that the tenancy can only be terminated by the landlords for a "just cause", which can mainly be on account of a fault of the tenant or because the landlord wants to occupy the property for himself/herself or for their family or if they wish to withdraw the property from the rental market or demolish/remodel it. This act also requires the landlord to pay for the relocation expenses of the tenant if the tenancy is terminated for no fault of the tenant.

Additionally, landlords cannot increase the rent payments as they wish. The maximum increase can be to the extent of 5% + the local Consumer Price Index. If the landlord does not increase the rent for a particular year, they cannot add the entitlement to the next year.

---

96. *Information on Deeds,* Website of the Los Angeles Registrar-Recorder/ County Clerk, https://www.lavote.gov/home/recorder/property-document-recording/forms/deeds

97. *Assembly Bill No. 1482, Tenant Protection Act of 2019,* Website of the California Legislature, https://leginfo.legislature.ca.gov/faces/billNavClient.xhtml?bill_id=201920200AB1482

9.3.3 Texas: Texas Occupations Code and Property Code[98]

Texas also provides for the licensing and qualification of real estate brokers and sales agents under Chapter 1101, Title 7 of the Occupations Code, calling it the Real Estate License Act.[99] Similar to California, Texas brokers and sales agents are also required to clear an examination and obtain a license in order to function. Here the license may only be valid for 24 months though and can be renewed for the same period. There are also continuing education requirements prescribed for brokers.

It also provides for the establishment of the Texas Real Estate Commission, to implement the rules of the Chapter. The commission has substantial powers to entertain complaints and carry out investigations. In addition, this Chapter provides for the establishment of a Texas Real Estate Broker-Lawyer Committee, which can prescribe contract forms to be used by brokers/sales agents for real estate transactions.

Texas regulates real estate transactions under Chapter 5 of Title 2 of the Texas Property Code, calling it the Uniform Vendor and Purchaser Risk Act. The law here is quite prescriptive in that it provides for an elaborate form of notice that a seller is required to provide, in relation to the condition of the property at the time of sale. In addition, a seller is required to disclose possible taxes and annexations, obligations related to membership in a property owner's association, or any obligations related to public improvement districts that may apply. It also provides for the form of a contract for conveyance (i.e. sale, transfer, etc.) of what it calls a "fee simple" estate in real property.

---

98. *Texas Constitution and Statutes,* Website of the Government of Texas, https://statutes.capitol.texas.gov/

99. *Occupations Code, Title 7, Texas Statutes,* Website of the Government of Texas, https://statutes.capitol.texas.gov/Docs/OC/htm/OC.1101.htm

Chapter 12 of the Property Code provides for the recording of instruments in relation to real or personal property in a tangible paper or electronic form by the county clerk.

Texas regulates landlord and tenant relationships under Chapters 91-94, Title 8 of the Texas Property Code.[100] It provides for the notice of termination of tenancies, separate provisions for residential and commercial tenancies, provisions relating to the landlord stopping a tenant from accessing the property, vacation of property by the tenant, charging penalties for late payment of rent, landlord and tenant remedies for violation, etc.

9.3.4 New York: Chapter 50 of the Consolidated Laws of New York[101]

New York regulates the intermediaries dealing with real estate transactions, conveyances, and recording of instruments through which real estate transactions are carried out through Chapter 50 of the Consolidated laws of New York.

Article 12-A of Chapter 50 of the Consolidated Laws of New York requires that in order to act as real estate brokers or salespersons, a license is required. In order to apply for a license, they are required to pass an examination and attend 75 hours of training in approved real estate courses.

New York also provides for disclosure by the seller to the buyer of real estate property prior to a sale, however, the prescribed disclosures are limited to the extent of facts such as:

---

100. *Property Code, Title 8, Texas Statutes,* Website of the Government of Texas, https://statutes.capitol.texas.gov/Docs/PR/htm/PR.91.htm

101. *Chapter 50, Real Property,* Consolidated Laws of New York, https://www.nysenate.gov/legislation/laws/RPP

- whether or not there is utility service provided in the property

- whether utility surcharges attach to the property

- if there are uncapped natural gas wells on the property

- whether a green jobs New York on-bill recovery charge applies to the property

[102]New York also provides for recording of conveyances in the office of the county clerk in which the property is situated. New York expressly provides that every conveyance which is not recorded in such manner is void against the person who subsequently purchases the same property in good faith and for valuable consideration. The county clerk where the conveyance is recorded is required to mail a notice of such conveyance to the owner of the record.

Landlord-tenant relationships in New York are governed by Article 7 of Chapter 50 and provide for remedies available to a tenant where the possession is not delivered, no retaliation by the landlord for legitimate complaints by the tenant, right to sublease or assign the property which is only available to the tenant with the consent of the landlord, specific provisions in relation to termination of contracts by senior citizens or victims of domestic violence, termination of tenancies at will, etc.

---

102. *Section 242, Article 8, Chapter 50, Real Property,* Consolidated Laws of New York, https://www.nysenate.gov/legislation/laws/RPP/242

9.3.5 Hawaii: Title 28 of Division 3 of Hawaii Revised Statutes[103]

Under the Hawaii Revised Statutes 2021, the regulation of real estate intermediaries and transactions is provided for in Title 25, Section 467 and Title 28, Section 501 onwards.[104]

Like the other states, Hawaii also requires real estate brokers and salespersons to clear an examination and secure a license before acting as such. Similarly, Hawaii also provides for the appointment of a Real Estate Commission which shall be responsible for granting the licenses and enforcing the provisions of the regulation of real estate licensees. It is also empowered to suspend, terminate or revoke any license belonging to the real estate brokers and salespersons.

Hawaii has relatively detailed provisions relating to mandatory seller disclosures in a contract of sale of real estate property. It provides that a residential property cannot be sold unless a disclosure statement as provided in Chapter 508D is provided to the buyer and the buyer acknowledges the receipt of the disclosure statement and is provided an opportunity to examine it.

Unlike the other states where deeds are recorded by the offices of county clerks, in Hawaii, the deeds are recorded with the Bureau of Conveyances, with a cover sheet and the necessary fees, depending upon the number of pages of the document being recorded.[105]

---

103. *Title 28, division 3, Hawaii Revised Statutes,* https://www.capitol.hawaii.gov/hrscurrent/Vol12_Ch0501-0588/HRS0501/HRS_0501-.htm

104. *Section 467, Title 25, 2021 Hawaii Revised Statutes,* law.justia.com, https://law.justia.com/codes/hawaii/2021/title-25/chapter-467/

105. *Website of the Bureau of Conveyances,* State of Hawaii, https://dlnr.hawaii.gov/boc/
www.vibrantpublishers.com

Hawaii also has a detailed landlord-tenant code, with detailed provisions relating to restrictions on the increase of rents for tenancies which are from month to month, provisions relating to what rental agreements should contain, such as the term of the tenancy, payment of attorney fees in case of a suit for unpaid rent, etc. The code also clearly provides for the obligations of the landlords such as providing the proper possession, maintaining the premises, clearly disclosing the persons authorized to manage the premises, etc. Tenant obligations provided for include an obligation to occupy and use the premises properly and inform the landlord about any defective condition of the premises of which the landlord may be unaware of.

Quiz

1. **The laws relating to real estate/real property can be found in:**

   a. The US Constitution

   b. The Uniform Commercial Code

   c. The Uniform Real Estate Act

   d. The state codes

2. **Most state codes provide that real estate brokers or salespersons must:**

   a. reside within the state of operation

   b. advertise themselves as real estate brokers or salespersons

   c. pass the appropriate exam and secure a license

   d. be at least 30 years of age.

3. **Most state codes provide that prior to a sale of real property:**

   a. a seller must make disclosures in relation to the condition of the property or any restrictions on it

   b. the buyer must make a payment for the property in one transaction

   c. the transaction must be approved by the relevant county clerk prior to execution

   d. the seller must ensure availability of utilities on the property

4. **The California Tenant Protection Act, 2019 provides that the landlord can terminate the tenancy:**

   a. at will - i.e. as and when desired by the landlord for any reason

   b. only for a "just cause"

   c. only upon a default in payment of rent by the tenant

   d. only after a period of six months

5. **The Fair Housing Act provides that:**

   a. the houses must be provided to customers at a fair price

   b. a fair return must be ensured to the developer for providing housing units

   c. there must not be any discrimination on account of race, colour, religion, etc. by housing providers

   d. housing loans should be provided by financial institutions for a fair interest rate

6. **The Fair Housing Act is administered by:**

   a. the Congress

   b. the Secretary of State

   c. the Secretary of Housing and Urban Development

   d. the county clerk/recorder

7. **Federal law contained in Title 43 USC deals with:**

   a. Landlord-Tenant Relationships

   b. public Lands

   c. community Development

   d. condominiums

8. **In Hawaii the conveyance for the sale of real property is required to be registered with:**

   a. the relevant county clerk/recorder

   b. registrar of the county

   c. Secretary of State

   d. bureau of Conveyances

9. **Public lands of more than 5000 acres can be withdrawn by the Department of Defense only with the approval of:**

   a. the President

   b. the State Senator

   c. Congress

   d. 75% of the public residing around the land

10. "Time-share" ownership refers to:

a. ownership by multiple individuals who have a right to occupy the vacation property for a specific time

b. ownership by landlords who rent the property for a specific period in a year

c. ownership of property in community development schemes which are only available at a specific time of the year

d. rent to buy ownerships

Answers	1 – d	2 – c	3 – a	4 – b	5 – c
	6 – c	7 – a	8 – d	9 – c	10 – a

Chapter Summary

◆ Real estate transactions tend to be more contract driven than regulated by law. There are no restrictions on what price someone should sell their property at. However, there are laws providing for disclosures in the sales of real property and recording such transactions.

◆ Real estate property transactions are regulated more at a state level than a federal level because the states are different in terms of area, availability of property, economics, etc.

◆ Federal law deals with public lands through Title 43 of the USC and provides for no discrimination in housing services through the Fair Housing Act.

◆ Most states have laws relating to the qualifications, examination, and licensing of real estate brokers and agents as well as provisions for setting up real estate commissions which are responsible for granting such licenses and regulating the licensees.

◆ The state codes also provide for disclosures by the seller regarding the condition of the property at the time of such sale. Texas provides a very descriptive form of notice in this regard.

◆ The state codes also provide for the recording of the conveyances with the relevant county clerk. In the case of Hawaii, the recording is required to be done with the Bureau of Conveyances.

◆ Landlord-tenant relationships are also regulated by the state codes, and these usually provide for the rights and remedies available to the landlords and tenants, restrictions on increases in rents, terminating the tenancy, etc.

This page is intentionally left blank

Chapter **10**

Tort Laws

A tort basically means a civil wrong: some injury or harm caused to a person because of an act or omission by another, which is not a criminal act. The person who has suffered the injury or harm can bring a civil suit against the person who caused such harm. The result of a suit i.e. the judgment is also in the form of a remedy or relief to the injured such as monetary damages or penalties.

After reading this chapter, you will be able to understand the following:

- What are tort laws and what kind of remedies do tort laws provide?

- What are the tort laws in the US?

- What is the difference between negligence and intentional torts?

- What is strict liability?

- What are personal injury claims and what do personal injury lawyers do?

- What is medical malpractice and what are the laws relating to medical malpractice?

10.1 What Are Tort Laws and What Kind of Remedies Do Tort Laws Provide?

Tort laws cover civil remedies that are made available to rectify the harm caused by a person's wrongful or injurious actions.

As we already noted, the primary aim of this law is to provide relief to a person affected by the harm caused and to deter others from committing such acts in the future. While tort law is broadly considered as a civil remedy, it is pertinent to understand that there may be instances wherein a tort committed may include criminal liability as well, for example, gross negligence committed by a person which endangers the lives of people may be considered as both, a tort and criminal negligence.

Tort law holds great significance in the US since there are several lawsuits instituted each year claiming relief against torts. There can be substantial damages awarded to people in the case of torts also. Tort law stems from common law and has developed over time via various precedents and interpretations made by judges. Several states have adopted their laws (in bits and pieces, to be precise) to govern lawsuits pertaining to tort, however, no all-inclusive codified law has been put in place yet.

In order to bring an action against someone under tort laws, an injury may not need to be physical. It may be emotional or it may include mental distress. Tort law may also include violation of privacy (privacy violation-related torts have been addressed by Restatement of the Law, Second, Torts, § 652).[106]

10.2 What Are the Tort Laws Prevalent in the United States?

As we discussed, tort laws usually stem from common law, and therefore, tort laws are formed out of judgment precedents. However, there are specific laws that relate to making governments liable for the tortious acts of their employees.

10.2.1 The Federal Tort Claims Act, 1946

Though there are no codified laws as such in the US, the Federal Tort Claims Act, 1946 (FTCA) is a federal legislation that was enacted to provide legal means to compensate individuals who have suffered a personal injury, death, or property loss or damage due to the negligent act or omission of an act by an employee of the federal government. This is subject to exceptions i.e. there are cases when the government would not be responsible for the acts of its employees. This act, thus, allows an injured person to recover damages from the US federal government.[107]

---

106. Yasmyne Ronquillo; Michael B. Pesce; Matthew Varacallo, *Tort*, Website of the National Library of Medicine,   https://www.ncbi.nlm.nih.gov/books/NBK441953/

107. *Federal Tort Claims Act*, Website of the United States House of Representatives, https://www.house.gov/doing-business-with-the-house/leases/federal-tort-claims-act

In addition to this, many states have their own tort claims acts in their codes or revised statutes, which were created to make the state liable for the acts of its employees. The basic intention here is to create an exception to the sovereign immunity granted to governments. However, both the federal and state tort claims act lay down an important exception: the governments are not liable for their employee's intentional torts.[108]

10.3 What Is the Difference Between Negligence and Intentional Torts?

Most tort cases in the US deal with negligence. It is therefore important to understand negligence and distinguish it from intentional torts.

10.3.1 Negligence

Negligence means a failure to act with a level of care that a person with an ordinary level of prudence would have exercised when put under similar circumstances. The said behavior consists of both action and an omission to act wherein there's a duty to act in a certain reasonable way.[109]

What is considered to be an ordinary level of prudence and whether someone's behavior lacks a reasonable degree of care would depend upon whether the person's conduct causing the

108. *State Tort Claims Acts,* biotech.law.lsu.edu, https://biotech.law.lsu.edu/map/statetortclaimsacts.html

109. *Definition of Negligence,* Legal Information Institute, Cornell Law School, https://www.law.cornell.edu/wex/negligence

harm was foreseeable and whether it could have been known how severe the harm would be and in view of that knowledge, would a reasonable person take precautions to eliminate or reduce the risk of harm.

For example, if in the process of packing some perishable products, it is known that the product is likely to be spoiled within a period of two days from the date of packing and there is no process to check if the "best before" date placed on the packaging is within the period of two days, this would fall within the category of negligence. This is because it is known that the product is likely to be spoiled and it is foreseeable that a person consuming such a product might fall sick. In such cases, if there is an omission to take the appropriate steps, it would be negligence.

A person suing for negligence would have to prove four elements to make a case against the defendant, *viz.*:

Existence of a duty to act

The defendant must have owed to the plaintiff a duty, which may be different in each case. It may include voluntary undertaking on behalf of the defendant to prevent the plaintiff from harm or it may also include instances wherein one may have knowledge of the fact that their acts may result in causing harm to the plaintiff.

For example, in our case related to edible products, there was knowledge of the fact that not ensuring the correct expiry date on the packaging can lead to an adverse effect on the health of the consumer.

Breach of duty

The defendant must have breached the existing duty.

The defendant's breach of duty is usually determined via the famous Hand Formula, formulated by Learned Judge Hand in the case titled *United States v. Carroll Towing*. Per the said formula, if **B<PL**, it shall be considered negligence by the party which was supposed to take reasonable precautions.

Here, B = burden of taking precautions,

P = probability of loss

L = gravity of loss

Hence, if the burden of taking precautions **(B)** is less than the probability of loss **(P)** multiplied by the gravity of any resulting loss **(L)**, then it would amount to negligence on behalf of the party which was entrusted with taking precautions. Simply put, this means that where someone could have easily identified the possibility of the loss and recognized how grave it would be and could have easily avoided the loss by taking some precautions, it would be negligence if they do not take such precautions.

Injury

There must have been an injury sustained by the plaintiff, which may either be bodily injury or a loss to property.

Injury must be caused by the defendant

The injury must have been caused by the defendant and there must be proof to this effect. Hence whoever claims negligence must not only prove that there was an injury to the plaintiff, but that the injury was caused by the defendant and that the injury was caused as a result of an act or omission of the defendant.

It is pertinent to mention herein that in certain circumstances, one may be liable for negligence caused by the acts of a third party also, for example, in cases where an employer may be held liable for the acts committed by an employee.

10.3.2 Intentional Torts

While negligence deals with acts or omissions which are below a standard level of care, intentional torts are clearly committed intentionally i.e. there is a clear intention to cause harm.

This type of torts, if proven, can result in the applicability of punitive damages. However, these types of torts are also difficult to prove, because it is not easy to know the mental state of the defendant at the time of the commission of the act. Hence unless such intention is clearly demonstrated by the act, it is difficult to prove that the tort was intentional.

An example of an intentional tort is "battery" - causing harmful or offensive contact to the person. This may also extend to causing harm to anything connected with the person such as their clothes. However, if this happens in a situation, where a person has consented by participating, then this would not be considered an intentional tort. An interesting example of this would be "bodyline" bowling in cricket which was intended to physically threaten the batsman.

Common intentional torts may include battery, trespass to land, trespass to chattel, false imprisonment, and intentional infliction of emotional distress.

10.4 Torts Giving Rise to Strict Liability

These torts are the torts in which a defendant is considered to be liable for any harm resulting to the plaintiff irrespective of whether the act was intentional or negligent. The view is that in cases of these torts, the defendant has been engaging in activities that are inherently dangerous and it would be known by the defendant that such activities carry a clear risk of causing harm to others.

There are mostly three kinds of conduct that may give rise to strict liability:

1. Possession of dangerous animals which are known to attack people or which have been previously known to attack visitors.

2. Engaging in abnormally dangerous activities (like activities that are not commonly undertaken and can cause harm to the person undertaking them), such as possessing firearms and leaving loaded firearms at places where these can be used by people who are prohibited from using them.

3. Product liability, which is one of the most prominent examples of strict liability.

10.5 Product Liability and Laws Applicable to Product Liability

Product liability refers to the liability of any/all of the parties along the manufacturing chain of a product for the damage caused by the said product. This would hence include each level of entities commencing from the top to the bottom of the manufacturing chain.

This liability can be considered a strict liability tort, however, in most cases, the burden of proof would be on the plaintiff. Product liability allows a plaintiff to recover damages from the seller in the event of receipt of a product that is dysfunctional/defective, which resulted in harm to the plaintiff.

Some of the types of defects which would result in product liability would be:

1. **Design defects:** In about 47 states, the plaintiff would have the burden of proof regarding the existence of a design-related defect whereas, in states like Alaska, California, and Hawaii, it is upon the defendant to prove that there exist no design-related defects.

2. **Manufacturing defects:** These are the defects caused during the manufacturing of an item.

3. **Marketing defects:** These defects comprise a lack of proper intimation to the buyer regarding the instructions pertaining to a product.[110]

10.5.1 Applicable Law

Since there is no federal product liability law, the United States Department of Commerce published the Model Uniform Products Liability Act (MUPLA) in 1979 which tried to encourage uniform laws for product liability. Nevertheless, the same has not yet been adopted widely.

---

110. *Definition of Products Liability,* Legal Information Institute, Cornell Law School, https://www.law.cornell.edu/wex/products_liability

Therefore, product liability can be dependent upon the precedents in different states and can be categorized either in the strict liability bucket or in the negligence bucket.

In most cases where a defective product was sold by a commercial seller, in order to prove a strict liability with regards to a product, a plaintiff would only have to prove that:

1. the defendant sold a product

2. the defendant was a commercial seller of the said product

3. the product was in a defective condition at the time of sale

4. the plaintiff, in view thereof, sustained an injury

5. it was the defect that actually and proximately caused the said injury to the plaintiff.

A jury will determine the product defect by using either a combination of the two tests or any one of the following tests:

1. **Consumer expectations test:** If a reasonable consumer, using the product in a reasonable manner would find the product defective, it is considered to be defective. If the defect is such that a reasonable person would not consider it to be defective, it will not be considered to be defective though it might not meet the standards that an expert would apply.

2. **The risk-utility test:** If there is a defect in the product which outweighs its utility, it is considered to be defective. However, if the utility of the product exceeds the defect, it would not be considered to be defective.

10.6 Consumer Protection Laws

There are a host of laws relating to consumer protection that are enacted at a federal level, however, the overarching law of all is the Consumer Product Safety Act (CPSA). This legislation established the Consumer Protection Safety Commission, an independent agency, defined its authority, and further allowed the agency to develop standards and bans. Furthermore, it allows the CPSC to pursue recalls and ban products under certain circumstances.

The CPSA specifies certain safety standards for the products for the ultimate safety of the customers. It can also provide for the ban and recall of products that are unsafe for consumers. The recall of a product would be implemented by the federal agency overseeing the category of product liable for recall.[111]

10.6.1 Bureau of Consumer Protection

The Federal Trade Commission (FTC) Bureau of Consumer Protection stops unfair, deceptive, and fraudulent business practices by collecting reports from consumers conducting investigations, and suing companies and people who break the law. They further develop rules to maintain fairness in the marketplace and educate people about their rights and responsibilities.

The FTC is also involved in creating awareness pertaining to the scams being initiated by scammers by means of spam calls. Furthermore, through their website, one can report such

---

111. *Consumer Product Safety Act,* Website of the United States Consumer Product Safety Commission, https://www.cpsc.gov/Regulations-Laws--Standards/Statutes

unwanted calls to the FTC. They even maintain a national do-not-call registry where one is free to register their house/work number.[112]

10.6.2 Personal Injury Claims

Personal injury claims can arise from a variety of injuries which may range from injuries to a person's body or injuries that may result from non-bodily harm like defamation, false imprisonment, etc.[113]

One of the most well-known cases for tort law (personal injury) is the *McDonald's hot coffee case* or *hot coffee case.* In the case titled, *Liebeck v. McDonald's*, a woman aged about 79 years ordered hot coffee from McDonald's which spilled on her and caused her to suffer third-degree burns leading to her hospitalization. It was estimated that the coffee was kept at up to 180-190 degrees to stay hot which is capable of causing serious harm to a person (within a matter of mere seconds), in the event it spills. Liebeck wanted to settle, however, owing to resistance from McDonald's, she took it to court wherein she was awarded compensatory damages of $200,000 which was thereafter reduced to $ 160,000 *(since the jury found her partially at fault)* and $2.7 million in punitive damages, which was thereafter reduced to $480,000. The parties thereafter entered into a post-verdict settlement.

There are generally three grounds based on which a personal injury claim may be sought:

---

112. *Bureau of Consumer Protection,* Website of the United States Federal Trade Commission, https://www.ftc.gov/about-ftc/bureaus-offices/bureau-consumer-protection

113. *Meaning of Personal Injury Recovery,* Legal Information Institute, Cornell Law School, https://www.law.cornell.edu/wex/personal_injury_recovery

1. **Negligence** – by acts or omission of acts that require standard care

2. **Strict liability** – which holds a person liable for their acts, irrespective of their mental state at the time of the commission of an act.

3. **Intentional wrongs** – resulting from intentional acts of defendants

Events in which personal injury may be claimed are similar to how any tort lawsuit is initiated, viz. there is an existence of a duty that is breached owing to an act or omission of an act by the defendant that thereby causes an injury to the plaintiff and there is a sufficient connection between the injury caused and the breach.

Some of the actions (non-exhaustive list) for which one may claim action under personal injury would be:

- Automobile accidents

- Workplace accidents

- Assaults

- Product defect accidents

- Nursing home abuse

- Intentional infliction of emotional distress

- Defamation

- False detention, arrest, or imprisonment

- Malicious prosecution

- Invasion of privacy

What do personal injury lawyers do?

Personal injury lawyers are specialized in the field of tort law and they assist their clients concerning the injury suffered by them. A specialized lawyer in this field brings to the table knowledge and experience about this law and therefore can advise their clients efficiently on how to proceed in such matters.

Such lawyers help their clients in recovering financial compensation for the loss suffered due to the tort committed by another. They would hence, help in the investigation of claims, gathering evidence, negotiating with the other parties, preparation of pleadings, conducting discovery (by sending interrogatories to the defendant asking for certain information, deposing the parties, and deposing witnesses), representing the client at trial, assessment of damages and in the entire variety of legal processes which one may have to go through if one suffers personal injury.[114]

10.6.3 Medical malpractice claims

Medical malpractice is covered within negligence in the US. Lawsuits claiming medical malpractice are quite common and hence, physicians are often required to maintain insurance against such claims.

How to prove medical malpractice

In order to prove medical malpractice, the injured patient must establish that the physician acted negligently while rendering care to them, and owing to such negligence, the patient suffered an injury. In view thereof, four elements must be proven:

---

114. Nidhi Bajaj, *All you need to know about personal injury lawyers and their work*, blog. ipleaders.in, https://blog.ipleaders.in/all-you-need-to-know-about-personal-injury-lawyers-and-their-work/

1. **Professional duty owed to the patient:** It comes into play as soon as a professional relationship is established between the health care provider and the patient. The idea here is that a doctor owes a duty to provide care to their patient while exercising reasonable care. This element may be the easiest one to establish considering one can easily prove duty whenever a doctor would assume the care of a patient.

2. **Breach of the said duty:** This can be proven by showcasing a breach of the standard of care that a doctor must have exercised while handling their patient. Though the standard of care may differ from state to state, depending upon their laws, the basic concept of the same may apply which is defined above. Some breaches of duty may be so obvious that they may need no specific proof. In the event of such apparent breaches, the jury may proceed to abridge the trial by determining the damages right away.

3. **Injury caused owing to the said breach:** Here, the patient has to establish a direct relationship between the breach of duty and the subsequent suffering of an injury by the patient.

4. **Resulting damages:** This is the final step of a medical malpractice lawsuit. Courts generally award monetary damages as compensation to the patient. Punitive damages are rare and would only be awarded if a grave mishap has occurred and the courts would then have a particular interest in deterring others from following the same unethical practice. For example, if a health care provider indulges in sexual misconduct against a patient or destroys a patient's medical records deliberately, etc.

Medical malpractice is hence, a subset of negligence, as discussed above wherein one has to prove similar elements when one institutes a lawsuit of negligence against another.

Cases where medical malpractice cannot be claimed

In cases of healthcare service providers who provide voluntary assistance to an injured or ill person, for example when there is an accident and a medical practitioner attends to the victim. This exception is required to ensure that medical practitioners attend to injured people in need of immediate help. While in general, it is not mandated to provide reasonable assistance to an injured person at the site of an emergency, certain states like Vermont & Minnesota specify a duty to provide reasonable assistance in the event of an emergency and one may satisfy this duty by reaching out for assistance by dialing 911.[115]

Applicable Law

In the US, medical malpractice has been under the regulation of respective states, instead of the federal government. Each state has its law and no unified law has yet been enacted in the US. Some states, via their law, have even capped a limit over the amount that can be recovered via damages in a lawsuit about medical malpractice. States like Alabama, Arizona, Arkansas, Georgia, Kentucky, Missouri, New Hampshire, Oregon, Pennsylvania, Washington, and Wyoming have no limitations over damages that can be recovered from a defendant in a medical malpractice lawsuit. Florida has capped the amount which can be recovered

---

115. B. Sonny Bal, *An Introduction to Medical Malpractice in the United States,* Website of the National Library of Medicine, https://www.ncbi.nlm.nih.gov/pmc/articles/PMC2628513/#:~:text=Medical%20malpractice%20is%20defined%20as,that%20deals%20with%20professional%20negligence

via limitations, however, there exist no limitations in medical malpractice which resulted in wrongful death.[116]

---

116. *Research and Policy,* Website of the National Conference of State Legislatures, https://www.ncsl.org/research/financial-services-and-commerce/medical-liability-medical-malpractice-laws.aspx

Quiz

1. **The Federal and State Tort Claims Acts intend to:**

    a. lay down the entire law relating to torts

    b. provide a distinction between torts at a federal level and torts at a state level

    c. provide an exception to sovereign immunity by making the governments liable for the acts of their employees

    d. lay down a formula for determining compensation for tortious acts

2. **Which of the following is an intentional tort?**

    a. Missing placing validity stickers on perishable goods

    b. Trespassing on someone's land

    c. Possessing firearms

    d. Failing to maintain medical records of patients

3. **The torts relating to privacy violations are contained in:**

    a. the Federal and State tort claims acts

    b. the Consumer Protection Safety Act

    c. the Model Uniform Product Liability Act

    d. the Restatement of the law, Second, Torts

4. **Which formula is used to determine breach of duty in negligence cases?**

   a. The arms length formula (B = P + L)

   b. The hand formula (B<PL)

   c. The hand-to-mouth formula (B>PL)

   d. The handshake formula (B>P + L)

5. **Which of the following would lead to strict liability?**

   a. Possessing dangerous animals

   b. Provoking someone to cause harm to another person

   c. Stalking someone

   d. Bursting firecrackers

6. **Against whom can a product liability case be instituted?**

   a. The manufacturer only

   b. Any of the parties in a manufacturing chain

   c. The distributor only

   d. The retailer only

7. **A consumer expectations test in relation to the product liability relates to:**

   a. whether a consumer would prefer the product compared to others

   b. whether a reasonable consumer would use the product in a specific manner

   c. whether the consumer would be willing to pay a specific price for the product

   d. whether a reasonable consumer, using the product in a reasonable manner would find the product defective

8. **Which of the following can provide for the ban or recall of a product?**

   a. The Bureau of Consumer Protection

   b. District courts, in a case against the manufacturer

   c. Consumer Protection Safety Commission

   d. Chambers of Commerce

9. **Which of the following cases would not amount to battery even when there is harmful contact?**

   a. When such harmful contact is conducted on a parent by a child

   b. When such harmful contact is conducted on a child by a parent

   c. When there is an implied consent for possible harmful contact such as participation in sports

   d. When such harmful contact is in response to another harmful contact

10. **In which of the following cases can medical malpractice not be claimed?**

    a. When the healthcare practitioner has professional indemnity insurance

    b. When the healthcare professional is voluntarily attending to someone who needs immediate medical attention

    c. When the healthcare practitioner is working at a government hospital

    d. When the healthcare professional is operating a private clinic

Answers	1 – c	2 – b	3 – d	4 – b	5 – a
	6 – b	7 – d	8 – c	9 – c	10 – b

Chapter Summary

◆ Torts are civil wrongs and tort laws provide civil remedies, mostly in the nature of a fine or monetary compensation.

◆ Most of the tort-related laws in the US have developed from judgments and precedents and there is no one codified law of torts applicable to all the states.

◆ Tort laws can deal with negligence, which is basically a failure of a duty to care, and intentional torts where there was an intention to cause harm.

◆ In certain circumstances, torts can invite strict liability, which means that the person who causes the harm would be liable, irrespective of whether the harm is caused by negligence or in an intentional manner.

◆ Claims related to product liability can arise where there are defects in the product that caused the harm and certain other conditions are fulfilled.

◆ There are a host of consumer protection laws in the US at a federal level, but the overarching law is the Consumer Product Safety Act.

◆ Personal injury claims can arise from harm caused to a person's body or even in the case of non-bodily harm.

◆ Medical malpractice claims are common in the US, but they require proof of similar characteristics like negligence.

Chapter 11

Basics of Securities Laws and Regulation of Capital Markets

A business requires funds to meet various expenses of operations. Some businesses are able to sell and meet the expenses from the sales proceeds themselves and do not require any further capital. These are known as "bootstrapped" businesses. However, a vast majority of businesses require additional funds in order to grow and therefore, these businesses are required to approach external sources or investors who can take the risk of investing in the business. There are other ways also in which a business can secure funds, such as loans. But in the initial stages, businesses usually do not have anything to offer to a lender as a security, and therefore, most investments in the initial stages tend to be towards the capital. When investors invest in the business in different ways, they are given "securities" in return for their investment.

In this chapter, we will learn the following:

- What are "securities"?

- What are "capital markets"?

- Why is there a need for securities laws?

- What are the major federal securities laws prevalent in the US?

- What are corporate governance and corporate responsibility and what are the laws relating to these in the US?

- Who are intermediaries in capital markets and what are the laws regulating intermediaries in the US?

11.1 What Are Securities?

Usually, in business, the word "security" is used for something that is provided as a safety measure to a lender, just in case a borrower fails to repay a loan. For example, someone can deposit a gold ornament with a lender as security or assurance of repayment to obtain a certain loan. When the loan is repaid, the "security" is handed back to the borrower. However, when the investment is not in the form of a loan, but as capital for a business, the investor is given a "share" of the business as a security instead of physical assets like gold ornaments. In order to enable the selling of a part of this share of a business, it is divided into units of uniform value known as "shares". Shares are the most common type of securities.

In addition to shares, there can be other types of securities such as bonds or debentures, which reflect debt or derivative securities such as futures and options. The definition of securities as provided in the Securities Act is very broad and includes many different types of securities.

However, generally, securities can be understood to mean transferable interests in a business.

11.1.1 What are capital markets?

A market is a place where buyers and sellers come together. Capital markets are therefore places where people who can invest capital and people who require capital come together. This means that businesses that require capital can offer their shares and investors who want to invest can buy those shares. Since the shares are not physical, the markets are also not at a specific physical location but are rather platforms.

A primary capital market arises when a business opens up and offers its shares to the public for the first time i.e. comes out with an IPO. A secondary market arises when the shares which are already held by people are bought and sold i.e. a stock exchange.

11.1.2 Why is there a need for securities laws?

Without regulation, the greed of people can result in the flourishing of a lot of ponzi investment schemes, which will result in people losing money and losing faith in investments. This is especially true where the investment is made by retail investors who do not have either the information or expertise to calculate the risks and returns of investment.

Securities laws, in some cases, therefore require investors to be "accredited", which would mean that these investors are seasoned and very well informed about the risks of investing as well as have more than adequate funds so that their lifestyle will not be affected even if they lose their entire investment.

Securities laws are also required to ensure the protection of investors, to keep the issuers of securities from spreading false information about the investment, require the risks in the investment to be disclosed clearly, and limit investment by the general public to cases that are not high risk.

11.2 Major Federal Securities Laws Prevalent in the United States

Securities laws in the US have been enacted at both federal and state levels and accordingly, compliance is also required at both levels. The state securities laws which require the filing are known as "blue sky laws". However, the federal securities laws are more relevant for issuers and therefore, we will discuss these.

11.2.1 Securities Act, 1933[117]

This is the most important legislation on securities. It defines all the basic concepts around securities such as securities themselves, who are issuers, what is an "offer" of securities, etc.

We already noted the meaning of the word "securities".

117. *Securities Act of 1933,* Website of the U.S. Government Information, https://www. govinfo.gov/content/pkg/COMPS-1884/pdf/COMPS-1884.pdf

www.vibrantpublishers.com

"Issuers" are companies who are looking to sell their securities. The basic concept of an "offer" is important to understand as it is when a company is looking to invite the public in general to buy its securities. Such transactions are regulated because the public interest is at stake since retail investors can be applying their hard-earned money to purchase such securities.

The Securities act requires registration of securities or sale of securities. The intention is to ensure that adequate information is available to the persons who purchase the securities so that they can take an informed decision as to whether or not to invest in the securities.

However, not all types of transactions are required to be registered. The Securities Act also provides for the exemption of certain transactions such as private placements (offering of securities privately to identified people) up to a certain number of people. Securities issued by the municipal, state, and federal governments are also not required to be registered. Nevertheless, there are still requirements in certain cases to file forms in order to claim the exemption from registration.

11.2.2 Securities Exchange Act, 1934

This act created the Securities Exchange Commission (SEC) which is basically the federal securities regulator for the US. The SEC has the authority to regulate the transactions in securities as well as the intermediaries in the securities market and self-regulatory organizations such as certain stock exchanges and even the Financial Industry Regulatory Authority (FINRA).

The Securities Exchange Act provides for the registration and regulation of stock exchanges, brokers and dealers, transfer agents, and clearing agencies. This is important because these intermediaries can lead people to believe that the securities are worth more than they actually are since they are paid to create a market for the securities. Further, they deal in the market on behalf of the retail investors and therefore they need to have the appropriate systems in place. The regulation is therefore required to prohibit fraud and misrepresentation.

Further, this act requires companies with more than $10 million in assets whose securities are held by more than 500 investors to make certain annual and periodic disclosures which are available on the SEC's Electronic Data Gathering, Analysis and Retrieval (EDGAR) system, so that people can track the changes in the company in which they have invested.

Additionally, this act also provides for two more important things - acquisition of securities i.e. when someone is looking to acquire more than 5% of the securities of a company by means of an offer for directly purchasing these securities from the current holders, they need to make certain specific disclosures. It is important that the existing owners of a company get to determine when the control of a company is changing hands i.e. when an external person is coming in and purchasing a large chunk of the company to take over the control and force the existing shareholders to sell their shares.

Such kinds of approaches are called "raiding" and there have been instances where such raiders have simply come in, acquired control over the shares of the company, and thereafter, instead of increasing the business of the company, have stripped the company into parts and sold off the parts to other businesses, thus gradually reducing the value of the shares and forcing the existing shareholders to sell at low rates.

The other important matter is insider trading. People who have inside information about the business of the company such as the management of the company, senior executives, and others who are involved in the strategic decision-making for the company have a better idea about how the price of the publicly traded shares of the company will move. They, therefore, gain an unfair advantage compared to the general public and can therefore benefit at the cost of the general public. They are therefore prohibited from dealing in the shares of the company at the time when they are in possession of such price-sensitive information. Insider trading is considered a serious crime and is subject to heavy penalties.

11.2.3 Securities Exchange Commission Rules and Regulations[118]

These rules and regulations provide for the organization of the SEC, the officers of the SEC such as the Chief Operating Officer, Secretary, Inspector General, etc., functions and powers of the SEC such as to make rules, to carry out investigations, etc. These also provide for the procedures to be carried out by the SEC, the prescribed forms, the manner of carrying out the investigations, collection of debt, etc.

11.2.4 Trust Indenture Act

This act requires entering into an agreement when debt securities such as bonds or debentures are issued, in addition to the requirement of registration of such securities. Such an agreement must also meet the requirements of this act.

---

118. *Rules and Regulations of the Securities and Exchange Commission and Major Securities Laws,* Website of the U.S. Securities and Exchange Commission, https://www.sec.gov/about/laws/secrulesregs

11.3 Corporate Governance and Corporate Responsibility

Corporate governance simply means the systems and processes used to run the business of a company in a manner that is transparent and is in the direction of the achievement of the objectives of the business. Corporate governance requires that the management functions in a manner that is in the best interests of the business and the shareholders.

Corporate responsibility, on the other hand, relates to the corporation giving back to the society, the environment, or the economy in some form.

11.3.1 Laws relating to corporate governance

Although corporate governance is more a matter of self-regulation i.e. businesses should be practicing corporate governance without it being imposed by law, there are certain laws in existence that require adherence to certain corporate governance practices.

Dodd-Frank Wall Street Reform and Consumer Protection Act ("Dodd-Frank Act")

The Dodd-Frank Act was an outcome of the 2008-2009 subprime lending crisis - a crisis caused mainly due to mortgage-backed lending by banks without appropriate checks on repaying capacities, which resulted in failure of large institutions in the US and impacted a lot of other countries. It drove many countries into recession, resulting in the loss of a lot of jobs and adversely impacting the lives of a lot of people.

The Dodd-Frank Act constituted a few authorities:

Financial Stability Oversight Council (FSOC)

This council is responsible for monitoring any risks to the financial stability of the US economy from the activities of the financial institutions such as large interconnected banks or non-banking finance companies whose failure is likely to adversely affect the economy. In addition to monitoring the activities, the FSOC basically promotes market discipline. Large financial institutions may function without appropriate governance mechanisms and internal checks since the underlying belief is that these are "too big to fail" and that they will always be backed by government action in the event of their failure because the public interest involved is too significant. However, the FSOC eliminates any such kinds of expectations by monitoring their activities. The FSOC also acts to identify potential threats to the US financial system.

Orderly liquidation authority

The orderly liquidation authority is actually a fund funded by large bank institutions and non-bank systemically important financial institutions. This fund is created from the money lent by the treasury to the Federal Deposit Insurance Corporation (FDIC) and the FDIC then recovers the money by imposing a fee on the existing large complex financial institutions.

Consumer Financial Protection Bureau

The Consumer Financial Protection Bureau is charged with overseeing financial products which are offered to customers to prevent financial harm to them and to educate and empower them on financial topics.

Volcker rule and restriction on derivatives

The Volcker rule relates to restricting how banks can invest and restricts speculative trading and prevents banks from being involved with hedge funds which are considered risky. It also provides for regulating derivatives, which were responsible for the 2008 subprime crisis.

Sarbanes-Oxley Act

The Sarbanes-Oxley Act was enacted in response to the corporate frauds at large corporations like Enron. It incorporates provisions requiring senior corporate officers to certify that the financial statements comply with the disclosure requirements of the SEC and requires that management and auditors establish internal controls and reporting methods to ensure the adequacy of controls. It also provides for specific record maintenance.

11.4 Intermediaries in the Capital Market

Some of the intermediaries in the capital markets are:

Broker-dealers: A broker-dealer is a person involved in the business of buying and selling securities either for their own selves or on behalf of their customers.

Clearing house: A clearing house is an intermediary which is formed to facilitate the exchange of payments, securities, or derivative transactions.

Transfer agents: Transfer agents are entities that are engaged in processing the transfer of shares for different companies.

11.4.1 Laws relating to the regulation of intermediaries

Investment Advisers Act

A person is categorized as an investment adviser if the person is providing advice in the business of securities and receives compensation for it. The Investment Advisers Act requires investment advisers to register under the Act with the SEC and provides for the procedure for registration, compliance, and ethical responsibilities.

Quiz

1. **Which of the following is not debt security?**

    a. Debentures

    b. Bonds

    c. Certificates of Deposit

    d. Preferred shares

2. **A private placement means:**

    a. issuing preferred shares at a specific place

    b. issuing shares only to the spouses of the founder

    c. issuing shares only specifically to certain identified persons

    d. transfer of shares by a founder to his or her spouse

3. **The securities regulator for the US is:**

    a. Financial Industry Regulatory Authority

    b. Secretary of State

    c. Securities Exchange Commission

    d. Internal Revenue

4. **Securities issued by which of the following are not required to be registered?**

   a. Startups

   b. Municipal, state, and federal governments

   c. Hospitals

   d. Schools

5. **Which of the following companies are required to make periodical disclosures to the SEC?**

   a. Companies with a net worth of $100 million

   b. Companies with a turnover of more than $100 million with at least 200 investors

   c. Companies with assets of more than $10 million with more than 500 investors

   d. Companies with a net worth of $50 million with at least 200 employees

6. **The Dodd-Frank Act was a result of:**

   a. the Enron crisis

   b. the Bernie Madoff Scam

   c. the subprime lending crisis

   d. the Theranos scam

7. **Which of the following is charged with overseeing financial products?**

   a. Consumer Financial Protection Bureau

   b. Securities Exchange Commission

   c. Financial Stability Oversight Council

   d. Orderly Liquidation Authority

8. **Transfer agents are the ones who:**

   a. are engaged in handling the share transfer on behalf of the company

   b. are engaged in the acquisition of businesses

   c. are engaged in the transfer of assets

   d. are the agents of an acquirer

9. **In which cases does an acquirer need to make disclosures?**

   a. Only when more than 25% of the shares of a corporation are being acquired

   b. When more than 5% of the shares of a company are being acquired by an offer

   c. When 75% of the assets of a company are acquired

   d. When an acquirer acquires, together with other people at least 30% of the publicly traded shares of a company

10. Insider trading means:

a. dealing in shares within the family

b. sale of shares to a spouse

c. dealing in shares by persons who have access to unpublished price sensitive information

d. trading between companies in the same group

Answers	1 – d	2 – c	3 – c	4 – b	5 – c
	6 – c	7 – a	8 – a	9 – b	10 – c

Chapter Summary

◆ Securities mean transferable instruments which can be bought and sold such as shares, bonds, etc.

◆ Securities laws exist at federal and state levels, but the ones at federal levels are important. The state-level securities laws are known as blue sky laws.

◆ Major federal securities laws include the Securities Act, Securities Exchange Act, Transfer Indenture Act, and other securities laws and regulations.

◆ Corporate governance means the systems and processes used to run the business in accordance with its objectives. Corporate responsibility on the other hand amounts to giving back to the society, the environment, or the economy.

◆ The laws relating to corporate governance can include the Dodd-Frank Act and the Sarbanes-Oxley Act.

Chapter **12**

Bankruptcy Laws

At the very core of any business, there is risk. If a business is successful, it can bring unprecedented wealth to its owners, but if a business fails, it can put the owners in the throes of deep debt. In order to be business-friendly, therefore, the laws of a country must not only ease the starting of a business but also its closing down.

Where a business has not been able to succeed, the laws must facilitate a fast resolution between a business and its creditors, thereby enabling the founders and creditors to arrive at a closure and move forward with their lives for other ventures or investments. Investors prefer to invest in countries that have faster bankruptcy resolution procedures for this reason.

After reading this chapter, you will be able to understand the following:

- What are the laws relating to bankruptcy in the US?

- When can an individual be declared bankrupt?

- When can an entity be declared bankrupt?

- What is the procedure to be followed for resolution?

- What are the consequences of being declared bankrupt?

12.1 Laws Relating to Bankruptcy in the United States[119]

The basic intention of bankruptcy laws in the US is to enable individuals or businesses who are overburdened by debt to close that chapter of improper financial management and make a fresh start in life or business. Instead of having debt cases drag on for a very long period of time without any resolution, it might be advantageous even for a creditor, to recognize exactly how much the debtor can pay and what part of the debt would be irrecoverable and required to be written off. The creditor can also then focus on other businesses rather than wasting time and energy on a debt that is not going to be recovered.

12.1.1 The Bankruptcy Code

Title 11 of the United States Code contains the Bankruptcy Code for the US and contains provisions relating to liquidation in Chapter 7 of the title and reorganization in Chapter 11 of the title, among other things. The Bankruptcy Code is the basic law that

---

119. *Bankruptcy Process, Bankruptcy Basics,* Website of the United States Courts, https://www.uscourts.gov/services-forms/bankruptcy/bankruptcy-basics/process-bankruptcy-basics

governs the provisions relating to bankruptcy. The substantive law relating to both individual and entity-related bankruptcy is covered in the Bankruptcy Code. The part relating to liquidation deals with both individuals and entities while the part relating to reorganization deals only with entities. For individuals, Chapter 13 further deals with adjustment of debts in cases of individuals who have a regular income.

There are other chapters dealing with the adjustment of debts for a municipality and the adjustment of debts for a family farmer or a fisherman, but we will not be discussing these here since they are applicable only in specific cases.

12.1.2 The Bankruptcy Rules and Local Rules

The procedural law in relation to bankruptcy can be found in the federal and local bankruptcy rules. Each of the bankruptcy courts in the 90 bankruptcy districts has its own officials and procedures to deal with bankruptcy as well. There are clearly established forms that are used under these rules.

12.1.3 The Bankruptcy Abuse Prevention and Consumer Protection Act of 2005

This act brought certain reforms in the bankruptcy procedures such as instituting a "means test" for the debtors in the case of bankruptcy applications under Chapter 7 to ensure that the bankruptcy applications are not abused by the debtor, just to get rid of the debt without facing any genuine struggle.

While bankruptcy provisions enable debtors to obtain a discharge of their debts and have a fresh start, it is not intended to allow everyone to create debts and then get them discharged by abusing the bankruptcy provisions. That is the purpose of instituting the means test. This analysis would have to be made by the attorney of the debtor, the clerk of the court, and the bankruptcy trustee.

This act also changed the appellate structure for bankruptcy cases among other changes.

12.2 When Can An Individual Be Declared Bankrupt?

Bankruptcy basically means the inability to pay debts. Interestingly, there is no specific time period prescribed for which a debt must be overdue in order for an individual to file for bankruptcy voluntarily. In general, when an individual finds himself or herself overburdened by debt and has to struggle continuously against being pursued by creditors for payment, being unable to generate enough income to make repayments and with suits filed by creditors to secure repayments, they can file for bankruptcy, in order to obtain a discharge of their debts.

There are no limits like a minimum or maximum amount of debt for which a bankruptcy petition can be filed voluntarily. However, you cannot file for bankruptcy under Chapter 13 if your total secured and unsecured debts exceed $2,750,000 as of the date of filing for bankruptcy relief.[120] Further, when an individual files a bankruptcy petition with the relevant bankruptcy court,

120. *Chapter 13 Bankruptcy Basics,* Websites of the United States Courts, https://www.uscourts.gov/services-forms/bankruptcy/bankruptcy-basics/chapter-13-bankruptcy-basics

the specific form (Form B-101) will provide all the details of the income, debts, etc. of the individual in order for the court to determine the inability to pay the debts. It is therefore not possible for a person to simply apply for bankruptcy and obtain a discharge of the debts for mala-fide purposes.

Bankruptcy is a serious matter and the petition cannot be filed lightly. It may enable an individual to obtain a discharge from the debts but might seriously hamper his or her ability to avail of credit again. Therefore, only individuals who face genuine difficulties with debt payments should file such a petition.

A petition for bankruptcy may also be filed against an individual by his or her creditors under Section 303 of the Bankruptcy Code if the debts are owed by such person to at least three creditors, and the amount of the debt owed is at least $10,000 more than the value of the property which is secured by such debts.[121] If there are less than 12 creditors (excluding certain types of creditors such as employees), then one or more of them can also file for bankruptcy if the debts owed to one or more of them exceed $10,000.

There are two more eligibility requirements for an individual to file a bankruptcy petition. The first one is that the individual should not have:

- wilfully failed to appear before a court or comply with the orders of a court in a previous bankruptcy filing 180 days prior to filing the bankruptcy petition; or

---

121. *11 U.S.C. Sec. 303, Involuntary Cases,* Legal Information Institute, Cornell Law School, https://www.law.cornell.edu/uscode/text/11/303

- voluntarily dismissed a previous case after creditors sought relief from court to recover property over which they held a lien.

The second one is that the debtor must have received credit counseling from an approved credit counseling agency at least 180 days before the submission of the bankruptcy petition. This is to ensure that the debtor does not repeatedly make the same mistakes, which lead to bankruptcy.

12.3 When Can An Entity Be Declared Bankrupt?

An entity can file for bankruptcy for exactly the same reasons as an individual - when an entity is overburdened by debts and is seeking relief in the repayment of such debts. However, the interesting part of an entity filing for bankruptcy is that an entity is considered to be a separate person from individuals and other entities. Therefore, even if one entity in the business group is highly profitable, another entity in the same group can still file for bankruptcy. This means that the ultimate owners of these companies can choose to obtain debt relief, even if at a group level, they might be capable of repaying the debts and do not really require help from the state to obtain debt relief.

One example of this is the strategy used by Johnson and Johnson which has come to be known as the "Texas two-step", after the name of the famous country style of dancing.[122] In this method, the two steps that are applied are that a large group like Johnson and Johnson will create an entity in business-friendly

---

122. *Definition of Texas Two-Step Bankruptcy,* investopedia.com, https://www. investopedia.com/texas-two-step-bankruptcy-definition-5225888

jurisdictions like Texas and transfer their liabilities (in this case, tort liabilities) to this new entity and then the new entity will file for a Chapter 11 bankruptcy voluntarily. These strategies, however, may not be in line with the spirit of the bankruptcy law and we may see new laws or judgments which can make these strategies illegal.

In the case of entities, most businesses will avoid filing for liquidating bankruptcy under Chapter 7 and prefer to file for reorganization under Chapter 11, since there is usually hope that once the business obtains some relief in the payment of its debts, it will be able to start afresh and generate profits. However, it is possible that during the proceedings, the bankruptcy court determines that it is no longer possible to reorganize the business, and therefore mandates the business to undergo a Chapter 7 bankruptcy.

In Chapter 11 bankruptcies, the business itself acts like a trustee, does not shut down, and continues to operate as usual - it needs to earn money in order to be able to repay its creditors. Businesses may also be successful in obtaining additional finances to repay their debts, known as "Debtor-in-possession" or DIP financing, which can help a business to reorganize and get back on track. The financier in this case obtains priority in repayment over the other lenders.

12.4 Procedure To Be Followed For Resolution

The procedures to be followed for the bankruptcy proceedings under Chapter 7, Chapter 11, and Chapter 13 are different. Let's look at the procedures for each different type:

12.4.1 Chapter 7

Following is the process to be followed for initiating the bankruptcy proceedings under Chapter 7:

Filing a petition

The first stage in a Chapter 7 process is the filing of a petition for bankruptcy. In addition to the petition, the debtor needs to file the following:

- A schedule of assets and liabilities

- A schedule of current expenditures and incomes

- A statement of financial affairs

- A schedule of executory contracts and unexpired leases

In addition, individual debtors must file a credit counseling certificate and a copy of a debt repayment plan which they have developed through credit counseling. Further, the details of the claims and amounts of the creditors, the debtor's income and property, and the debtor's normal living expenses. There are filing fees also required to be paid of over $300, but in the event that the debtor's income is below 150% of the poverty level, the court may waive the requirement for the fees.

Once such petition is filed, the creditor's proceedings are stayed.

Appointment of the Trustee

When a Chapter 7 petition is filed, the US Trustee or the bankruptcy court shall appoint an impartial trustee to administer the non-exempt assets of the debtor. Some of the states in the US have separate provisions for exempting assets of the debtor from being liquidated in Chapter 7 proceedings.

The main role of a trustee is to liquidate the assets of the debtor. The creditors must file their claims with the trustee.

The trustee will hold a meeting of the creditors within 21 to 40 days from the date of filing the petition and the debtor must be present in that meeting to answer the questions of the creditors. After the meeting, the US trustee shall make a report to the court as to whether the case can be considered an abuse under the means-testing norms of that state.

Often, the liquidation process does not take long, because the debtors usually have hardly any non-exempt assets. Most cases are therefore "no-asset" cases.

Discharge

A discharge means that the debtor is released from liability and although the discharge is subject to exceptions, the debtors receive a discharge in most of the cases. Unless an objection is filed, the debtor usually receives a discharge and the court will issue a discharge order.

12.4.2 Chapter 11

Businesses usually prefer to file for bankruptcy under Chapter 11, since with the risk, there is also the hope of being able to get the business back on track. Let's take a look at the process in brief under Chapter 11.

Filing of a petition

Like Chapter 7, the process of bankruptcy under Section 11 also begins with the filing of a petition and the schedules of assets and liabilities, expenditures and incomes, executory contracts and unexpired leases as well as the financial statements.

As soon as the bankruptcy petition is filed, three things take effect: all the actions by the creditors automatically stay, the debtor automatically assumes a fiduciary role with respect to the assets by itself as a "debtor in possession" and is permitted to carry on the business as usual. The regular activities of the business are not stayed. The US trustee is involved in monitoring the operations of the business, including the submission of the plans and disclosure statements.

Notice to the creditors and submission of proof of claim

The court clerk shall send a notice to all creditors who are scheduled. All creditors who are on a list or schedule of the debtors do not have to submit a proof, but any unsecured creditors who are not scheduled have to submit a proof of claim from the debtor. If the proof of claim is properly filed, it takes precedence over the schedule.

Creating a committee of creditors

A committee of creditors is created by the US Trustee, consisting of unsecured creditors who hold the seven largest unsecured claims against the debtor. The committee oversees the debtor's operation of the business and also helps to formulate a plan.

Submission of a plan of reorganization

The debtor may file a plan of reorganization within the first 120 days of the submission of the bankruptcy petition. However, the court can grant an extension of this period for up to 18 months from the date of filing the petition. The plan of reorganization will include a categorization of the claims and provide for a plan of how these claims will be dealt with.

Submission and approval of disclosure statement

The debtor is required to file a disclosure statement that has enough information and details to enable the holder of a claim to make an informed judgment about the plan. The debtor is required to secure approval of the court for the disclosure statement before there can be any voting or approval of the plan of reorganization.

Approval of the plan of reorganization by the creditors and confirmation hearing

The creditors will vote on the plan of reorganization and once approved, the plan will be submitted to the court for a confirmation hearing. The court will then view the plan in view of whether it is feasible, whether it is in good faith, and whether the plan proponent is in compliance with the requirements of the Bankruptcy Code. As regards the feasibility, the court shall form a view with respect to two aspects - that the plan is not likely to be followed by liquidation and that the plan will not require further financial organization.

Once a plan is confirmed, it amounts to discharging the debtor for any debt that arose prior to the date of such confirmation.

12.5 Consequences - What Happens in the Aftermath of Bankruptcy?

Once a discharge order is issued by a court in a Chapter 7 bankruptcy, the creditors will be prohibited from taking any action against the debtor and it results in the release of the debtor from personal liability for most of the debts.

A Chapter 11 bankruptcy, however, requires the implementation of the plan which has been confirmed by the court, and therefore, this is a process rather than a single point in judgment. Therefore, it will be seen that the plan is actually administered and that the payments are made in accordance with the plan. Once the entire plan has been implemented, a final decree would need to be entered for closing the case.

Quiz

1. The purpose of the bankruptcy law is to:

   a. ensure that nobody borrows beyond their means

   b. enable individuals or businesses overburdened by debt to make a fresh start

   c. enable creditors to recover the maximum amount possible

   d. clean up unviable businesses from the system

2. The primary legislation relating to bankruptcy is:

   a. Title 7 of the Uniform Commercial Code

   b. the Bankruptcies Act

   c. the Bankruptcy Code

   d. the Small Business Bankruptcy Act

3. An individual cannot file a bankruptcy petition if:

   a. the total debts outstanding are less than $30,000

   b. the individual has not undertaken credit counseling from approved credit counseling agency

   c. the debts were incurred on account of overspending by the individual

   d. the individual is still employed

4. **The "Texas two-step" is:**

   a. a famous judgment of the Texas bankruptcy court

   b. a legislation which enables bankruptcy petitions to be discharged in two steps

   c. a controversial bankruptcy strategy used by companies

   d. an established method of "means testing" used in Texas

5. **A "Debtor-in-possession" means:**

   a. debtors who possess real estate properties

   b. debtors can avail of additional funding to possess real estate properties

   c. debtors act in a fiduciary capacity as regards the assets and can carry on the business as usual

   d. debtors can arrange for their affiliates or connected persons to possess their properties

6. **In a Chapter 11 bankruptcy procedure, a _____ needs to be filed by the debtor within 120 days of the filing of the petition.**

   a. plan of reorganization

   b. plan of winding up

   c. plan of payments

   d. plan of business strategies

7. A committee of _____ is formed by the US trustee in the case of a Chapter 11 bankruptcy.

   a. bankers

   b. debtors

   c. trustees

   d. creditors

8. The creditors who are not in the schedule are required to file a _____

   a. plan of reorganization

   b. disclosure statement

   c. proof of claims

   d. final decree

9. The main role of a trustee in a Chapter 7 bankruptcy is to:

   a. create a committee of creditors

   b. review the documents submitted by the debtor

   c. arrange a meeting of the committee of creditors

   d. liquidate the assets and arrange disbursements

10. In considering the feasibility of a plan of reorganization, the court will consider:

a. whether the plan is likely to be followed by liquidation

b. whether the plan provides for at least 90% payments to the creditors

c. whether the business of the debtor can generate profits in the next three months

d. whether the business is likely to generate at least $100,000 in revenue

Answers	1 – b	2 – c	3 – b	4 – c	5 – c
	6 – a	7 – d	8 – c	9 – d	10 – a

Chapter Summary

◆ The primary legislation dealing with bankruptcy is the Bankruptcy Code, which is laid out in Title 11 of the United States Code.

◆ There is no time limit for a debt to be outstanding or a minimum amount of debt in order for a debtor to be able to file for bankruptcy voluntarily. However, where the bankruptcy petition is filed by creditors, certain minimum requirements need to be met.

◆ Bankruptcy filings would be checked under the means testing norms to ensure that the process of bankruptcy is not being abused to get rid of the debts wrongfully.

◆ Business entities can also file for bankruptcy if such entities are overburdened by debt. However, in the case of businesses, most businesses will prefer to file for a Chapter 11 bankruptcy procedure since this provides a chance to reorganize the payments and get the business back on track.

◆ Chapter 7 provides for liquidation, which means that the non-exempt assets of the debtor will be sold and the proceeds will be distributed among the creditors.

◆ Chapter 11 provides for a detailed procedure that ends with the confirmation of a plan of reorganization, which provides for the categorization of the claims and how these will be repaid.

◆ In both cases, individuals or businesses will be able to obtain a discharge from their debts and begin with a fresh start.

Notes